Shrink Your Handicap

Shrink Your Handicap

PHIL LEE, M.D., AND
JEFF WARNE

NEW YORK

Original hardcover design by Ruth Lee

Library of Congress Cataloging-in-Publication Data

Lee, Phillip
    Shrink your handicap / by Phillip Lee and Jeff Warne.—1st ed.
      p.   cm.
    ISBN 0-7868-6632-2
    1. Golf—Psychological aspects.   I. Warne, Jeff.   II. Title.
  GV979.P75 L44 2000
  796.352'6—dc21

Hyperion books are available for special promotions and premiums. For details contact Hyperion Special Markets, 77 West 66th Street, 11th floor, New York, New York, 10023, or call 212-456-0100.

99-055998

FIRST PAPERBACK EDITION

PAPERBACK ISBN: 0-7868-8554-8

10   9   8   7   6   5   4   3   2   1

In any round of golf there is a certain amount of luck, and this is true in life as well. I, myself, have been exceedingly lucky. My parents, my wonderful sister, my lovely and talented wife, Diane, and my children—Jennifer, David, and Jason—have given me tremendous happiness, while my loyal and hardworking clients have taught me as much about fun and accomplishment as I have been able to teach them.

—PHIL LEE, M.D.

This book is dedicated to my mother, April, my source of inspiration, perseverance, and determination. I would also like to thank my father Charles, my wife Cindy, and my children—Jessica, Lindsay, and Sam—who have patiently and selflessly supported my dreams.

—JEFF WARNE

Acknowledgments

WE THANK the very professional staffs of Atlantic Golf Club, Sleepy Hollow Golf Club, Scarsdale Golf Club, and Jim McLean and his staff at Doral for their generous assistance. Our superb editor at Hyperion, Gretchen Young, and the talented Jennifer Morgan were tireless in their efforts. Mark Reiter, our agent at IMG, and the able Michelle Yung were invaluable. We gratefully acknowledge the assistance of the art department at Troll Communications, especially Shi Chen and Steven Dolce. And, like everyone who has ever met her, we cannot thank Candy Lee enough.

▷ Contents

Authors' Note

ALTHOUGH ONE of the authors is left-handed, all references and all pictures are right-handed in orientation. The purpose is clarity, and of course no disrespect to the left-handed is intended. All left-handed people have a lifetime of experience translating instructions and descriptions; inclusion of phrases such as "when the hands are released early the ball will curve left for the right-handed golfer while curving right for the left-handed golfer" add nothing but an extra layer of prose. Similarly, while both authors work extensively with women golfers, the traditional usage is followed in this book (viz., "When the golfer feels threatened on the course by a hazard, he may react as if to a saber-toothed tiger, tightening his grip on the club."). The women who were kind enough to review sample passages felt that the more politically correct substitution of "she" for "he" or the alternating usage of "he" and "she" added an unnecessary layer of confusion to the book.

Introduction: Only Man Gets Anxious

THE LION seems to catch the gazelle every time. The monkey flips from limb to limb without hesitation. The eagle snatches the rodent. The seal catches the fish.

Does the monkey have a swing doctor? Does the lion have a sports psychologist? Of course not! They're doing what comes naturally. So far, so good.

But bring the animals closer to humans and the trouble starts. The thoroughbred horse has trouble getting out of the gate. The hawk won't leave the master's shoulder. And the bird dog, instead of hunting, seems to be having an anxiety attack.

Only man gets anxious. But as soon as we create artificial rules, even animals begin to experience difficulty. The more natural the sport, the less the psychological interference. Conversely, the more unnatural the sport, the larger the role assumed by anxiety.

Only man creates rules for how we should compete. We doubt if even the highest nonhuman life forms worry about who's away, or who's watching, or who can hit something the farthest.

You don't have to be a psychiatrist or a golf pro to figure out what the problem is for the troubled animals. They're not doing exactly what comes naturally. Something about their current situation is interfering with their innate ability to run, or fly, or sniff a trail.

Everyone knows that golf is a very unnatural game. And anyone who forgets that has only to watch a good athlete play golf for the first time to be reminded of just how unnatural and difficult a game it is.

But our purpose is not to stress how difficult it is to get better at golf or to extol some tedious format for self-improvement.

On the contrary, if we can transmit one message, it is that improvement in golf is often made more difficult than necessary.

Of course you want to get better. So what do you do? You add some swing change to your game. And over months or years you have the potential to improve. But why not improve today?

YOU ALREADY KNOW THE ANSWER

You already hit the ball significantly better on the range than on the course. You already hit the ball significantly better alone than in competition. Why add anything to your game?

Instead, why not subtract whatever changes when you go from the driving range to the course?

YOUR DRIVING RANGE GAME

When we say your "driving range game" we mean simply this: how well you hit the ball on the driving range or when you are alone on the course.

That's really how well you play. But wouldn't it be nice to be able to count on playing that well the rest of the time?

On the course there are many things that can make one anxious. Annette was the CEO of an Internet firm, and a gifted athlete. Although she had taken up golf relatively late in life (in her thirties), she was a contender for women's club champion. She came to us because part of her game had exploded. She could no longer hit out of sand. Her swing became tight and forced. She described herself as feeling like the tin woodsman looking for a can of oil.

Soon hitting over a trap filled her with fear. Her body would tighten up, her backswing would shorten, her hands strangled the club.

She was caught in golf's typical downward spiral. The more anxious she became, the more errors she made; and the more errors she made when faced with sand, the more anxious she became about the prospect of having to hit over it.

Our analysis revealed two problems. Annette was having a panic attack whenever she had to hit over sand, and Annette's technique for getting out of sand had a "balloon flaw."

There are many flaws in the golf swing, but most of them are pervasive. That means that they appear all the time, whether one is in an anxious situation or not. Twenty handicappers play like 20 handicappers when they are alone on the course. Five handicappers play like 5 handicappers when they are alone on the course. They don't usually look the same. But there are a few swing flaws, discussed in this book, that don't look the same when you are alone on the course and when you are in an anxiety-provoking situation. There are certain swing flaws that balloon when filled with anxiety. These flaws, and the anxiety that balloons them, kill your range game on the course.

Using cognitive and imagery techniques, which are made available to you in this book, we closed Annette's spigot of anxiety chemicals in one session. Her sand technique itself wasn't bad, but it contained one of the balloon flaws that is greatly amplified by the presence of anxiety. That flaw was fixed as is shown in Chapter 12 on sand play.

Bill is a managing director at a prominent investment house. A power hitter and advanced golfer who plays to a 4 handicap, Bill developed a tendency to slice in pressure situations when there was a hazard on the right. He noted the irony: He was hitting his ball in these situations exactly where he did not want it to go. Two sessions cooled the competitive anxiety, and two further sessions identified the balloon driving flaw on which the anxiety was preying.

There are many, many possible swing flaws, which is why there is a great deal of variety on how people play. But there are only a few swing flaws that typically and repeatedly balloon, becoming much more dangerous when there is anxiety present. The solution to those particular swing flaws, and to the anxiety that triggers them, is what this book is all about.

WHO ARE WE TO TALK?

Phil Lee, M.D., the golf psychiatrist:

> I was watching my own handicap balloon. I consulted Jeff Warne, the *GOLF Magazine* Top 100 teacher. A few technical changes and I dropped eight strokes from my handicap. Why? It's simple. There are specific swing weaknesses that are magnets for the chemicals of anxiety. Even the tiniest amount of anxiety produces chemicals that will feast on certain specific weaknesses in the swing.
>
> The essence of mental defenses is to dramatically reduce anxiety. I already knew how to convert many anxiety chemicals into few anxiety chemicals. What I learned from Jeff is how even these few chemicals affect the swing in predictable ways. Then I learned that these chemically induced swing changes can be nullified by appropriate physical countermeasures. The physical countermeasures to the effects of anxiety are easy to learn and are here in this book.

Jeff Warne, *GOLF Magazine* Top 100 teacher:

> I found myself for the first time in my life losing focus on the golf course. The more I berated myself for not paying attention to the shot, the harder I found it to concentrate. Tired of the downward spiral of

anxiety leading to poor shot leading to more anxiety, I consulted Phil Lee, the golf psychiatrist. After one thirty-minute session, I had my game back.

Anxiety on the golf course can be nullified by proper mental technique. Dr. Lee's techniques for killing anxiety before it kills your game are here in this book. There is no better feeling than the one you get when you are playing your range game on the course.

We teamed up to help other golfers, and out of our years of work together comes this revolutionary book.

When you are on the range, or on the course by yourself, then you are at your most natural. That is when you are most free to be yourself.

Bring in rules, bring in observation, bring in competition—and certain shots may change for the worse. This is natural: Even animals have problems with human rules. Fortunately, there is a solution. You can return to your natural game, your range game.

Only two things stand in your way. The first is your natural anxiety in these anxiety-provoking situations. This can be eliminated or drastically reduced by the techniques in this book.

Secondly, any amount of anxiety can attack certain swing flaws. Think about this: Most swing flaws are just that—swing flaws. No matter how many, or how few, people are watching, these swing flaws exert their influence. A 33 handicap doesn't look like a 6 handicap, even if no one is watching.

But there are certain swing flaws that have the capacity to grow. These flaws balloon under the pressure of anxiety. If you play badly alone and equally badly under scrutiny, then these specific swing flaws are not relevant to you.

However, if you play at a certain level, and that level is hard to attain in an anxiety-provoking circumstance, then these are the swing flaws you want to fix. Those swing flaws—the ones that balloon when pressurized by anxiety—are presented and corrected in this book. Anxiety, which is like the helium that inflates these swing flaws, is eliminated by this book. When you have dampened anxiety, and eliminated the swing flaws that balloon under its influence, then you are very close to having your range game with you on the course.

Before we wrote *Shrink Your Handicap*, we looked at some of the other golf titles available. There are many helpful treatises on the swing. If one surveys the popular titles it becomes clear that the public (rightly) does not want to wait to get better. There almost seems to be a competition among golf books to promise quick results. Jim McLean has the indispensable *Eight-Step Swing*. Ben Hogan gave us his *Five Lessons: The Modern Fundamentals of Golf*. Joe Dante proposes the interesting *Four Magic Moves to Winning Golf*. Carl Lohren ups the ante with *One Move to Better Golf*.

We reraise. We propose No Moves to Better Golf. We know that you don't need to add any moves to play better. Because you already do. When you are alone, or on the range, you play a better brand of golf. If you spend years improving your swing (which is a good idea if you want to put in the time) there will still be the gap between how you play on the range and how you play on the course.

Unless you close that gap, it will not matter how much better you get: The gap will always be there. You might as well close that gap now. The easiest and by far the quickest way to get better is simply this: Close the gap between your range game and your course game.

SECTION 1: *Why Is the Course Harder Than the Range?*

Golf Is Not a Mental Game

THE PHRASE "all men are mortal" is taught in schools as an example of incontrovertible truth, but, as Freud points out, no one ever really believes it.

The same is true of the statement "golf is a mental game."

Deep down we know this cannot be true, at least for ourselves. *Chess* is a mental game. *Scrabble* is a mental game. *Jeopardy!* is a mental game. Golf is a game of power and skill, and if we swing hard enough and well enough great things will happen.

And, in fact, this is true. But how do we explain the difference between the great things that happen relatively more often on the practice range and the great things that happen relatively less often on the course? How do we explain the difference between the great things that happen (sometimes) when we are alone on the course, and the not-so-great things that happen in the weekly foursome, or the club championship, or the tour event?

Golf is certainly a physical event. The only head I hit the ball with is on the end of my driver. But look at the surprising variations in results. When I tee up a postage stamp I almost never miss the letter. When was the last time you had to duck as the fork traveled toward the mouth? When we pass the salt we don't shout "fore!"

But even though golf is certainly a physical event, a great drive right down the middle and a hook to the left are also *both* physical events. And it often seems like which physical event pops up is dictated by circumstance.

Now, if the arms swing the club, and the club hits the ball, what has circumstance got to do with it? The ball doesn't know that you're playing with your boss. The club doesn't know that there are a lot of people on the first tee. Even your arms don't know that it's the 18th hole of an all-square match. But *you* know all this, and, in fact, you've been thinking about it for quite a while. You've got that feeling you get when you think about stuff like this. And, surprise, surprise, you're not hitting the ball the way you do on the range.

This book is about why that is, about what happens in your head, and what happens in your swing. And about what you can do to change all that.

After all, your golf ball is the same. And, unless you just bought new ones (again), your clubs are the same. If it's your home course, the fairways, bunkers, and greens are more or less the same.

Why should your head be different and, by extension, why should your shots be different? Why shouldn't you be as good out on the course as you really are?

HOW GOOD ARE YOU?

Well, that's a good question. And it has something in common with most good questions—the common answers are not entirely satisfactory.

The handicap system is the *statistical* answer to the question of how good you are and is basically the average of your score over a period of time. But does your handicap answer the question of how good you are? Of course not.

If we sit behind you at the driving range for a week and video-tape all your shots (and then cut out the occasional grounder or duck hook or wild slice), does that videotape represent how good you are? It better. Because that's as good as it gets.

If you're hoping for anything better than that, then take some lessons and prepare to practice.

But most people aren't hoping for anything better than that.

The problem for most people is that they are expecting, not something better than their range game, but just their *good* range game. That's all. It doesn't seem like too much to ask for.

But if it isn't too much to ask for, why doesn't it appear?

That's why people get mad. People are reasonable. People don't get mad because they didn't just hit a 370-yard drive. They've never been able to hit a 370-yard drive in their lives. People get mad because they know—from experience on the range—that they can hit this or that particular shot. And they just didn't.

That's what wraps clubs around trees.

Nobody wraps clubs around trees on the range. Nobody throws clubs in the pond, snaps a club over a knee, or even buries a club head in the turf on the range.

People don't even get sulky and irritable on the range (or when playing alone).

People don't start hoping that the other guys will whiff it on the range.

People don't start taking extra practice swings (or perhaps any practice swings).

The range is different. And the golf is better. So what exactly is the difference?

On the range we are simply trying to hit good shots. On the course, for a variety of reasons, we are *afraid* of hitting bad shots. Fear has a pronounced effect on our golf game.

THE NATURE OF FEAR

One million years ago we lived in caves. We'd wander out for a pleasant stroll and run into a saber-toothed tiger (now *that* is "a good walk spoiled"). Our eyes would dilate. Our breathing would quicken. Blood would be rerouted from our stomach to our arms and legs giving us extra strength to attack or flee. Our hearing would become more acute. Because our breathing quickened (to bring more oxygen to our arm and leg muscles), we would become a little light-headed (because we're blowing off carbon dioxide) and perhaps even numb and tingly, especially in the fingers and around the mouth. Because blood had been shunted from the stomach to the muscles we might feel slight nausea or have various unusual sensations of tightening in the chest and gut. We would have an overwhelming feeling of anxiety and fear, which would galvanize us into either fight or flight.

We'd swing our club at the tiger with all our strength for as long as we could swing it, or we'd run as fast as we could to the cave.

The anxiety/fear and the physical changes in arm and leg strength, breathing, sight, and hearing, as well as tension in the chest and gut, are all caused by chemicals that the body releases upon perceiving danger.

We're all descended from cavemen who had these chemicals. (Cavepeople who didn't have them stood around and were eaten by the tiger.) We need these chemicals. If you walk to your car and a mugger leaps out at you, then your heart will pound, blood will be shunted to your muscles for power, your breathing will quicken, and your eyes will dilate. This is an important reaction to be able to have. If someone threatens your life and you are perfectly calm, almost indifferent, afterward you will wonder: What is the matter? Why was I so shut down in the face of danger? On the other hand, if your heart pounds, your eyes dilate, your muscles tense, and you run to the precinct station or you fight back, you will feel (correctly) that that was a normal response and you will be happy you responded normally—quickly and instinctively.

But, if you step up to the first tee and your heart pounds and your muscles tense and your breathing quickens enough so you feel slightly disoriented—well, you will not be happy. But who has not felt this way?

The good news is that this is a perfectly natural, chemically mediated way to feel in the face of danger.

The bad news is that these chemicals are of absolutely no use in helping you escape from the hazards of a golf course.

To play your range game on the course you have to either eliminate the production of fear chemicals or make yourself immune to their effects. Both are possible when you understand what is going on.

HOW THE BRAIN WORKS

The brain is like a two-story house with a basement:

Upstairs

Here is everything we were taught by our parents, Sunday school, teachers. Everything related to *should* and *ought*. Like an off-limits section in a library: you can't go up there; you submit a card and after awhile a book comes down mostly censored. Everything with *should* and *ought* comes from the upstairs; all self-critical thoughts come from the upstairs: "Don't go in the water." "You ought to make this." "Don't mess up the tee shot." "You'll look like a dork if you three putt."

Basement

In the basement there is a caveman unchanged from one million years ago. (Yes, this is the primitive part of our brain.) The caveman wants to walk down Main Street and hit people over the head with a club, or drag women off to the cave, or break a window and steal a shiny necklace. Every exuberant or aggressive thought comes from the basement. On the golf course the caveman is saying: "Really whack it." "Don't leave anything on the table." "Let the big dog eat."

GROUND FLOOR

This is what we think of as *us*. This is the only part of our mind that we are consciously aware of, and the only part of our mind that is accessible to us.

This part examines our various options to select the best course of action. This is the part that says: Car coming at 60 miles per hour, 300 feet away—I can cross the street. This is also the part on the golf course that estimates how far it is over the water, and takes into account the left to right wind and the back right pin position. So far, so good. But . . .

This is also the part that evaluates the demands of Upstairs and Basement, and tries to find a compromise between them. (The Upstairs and the Downstairs may not pack the wallop of a speeding car, but they can make us, the Ground Floor, feel plenty bad if we don't listen to them.)

The Upstairs says: "Don't make mistakes." "Your partner is counting on you!" "People will think you're no good!" The Basement (caveman) says: "Go for it!" "Show them your stuff!" The Ground Floor wants to be logical and say, "This is 160 yards, let's use our 160-yard club." Obviously, the Ground Floor (us) is caught in the middle: It's hard to do both. It's very hard to *go for it* and *not make mistakes*. The more you go for it, the more likely you are to make mistakes. And conversely, the more careful you are to not make mistakes, the less you are going for it. If you're going to go for it, then it's a full 7 and you go over the trap. And if you're going to be sure of getting there, it's a 6 iron. But if you're going to be sure of getting there, you're also going to go for the accessible part of the green. Everybody is watching. If you swing freely (Basement), you could go Out of Bounds. If you try to control the shot and not look foolish (Upstairs), you won't necessarily be safe.

What is the Ground Floor supposed to do? How is the only part of our mind that we are aware of (the Ground Floor) supposed to respond to these internal threats, as well as to the other "saber-toothed tigers" of sand and water that threaten us? And speaking of threats, what about the audience (the rest of our foursome or the nationwide TV viewership) that will ridicule us? These internal demands, in addition to the external threats of the course, are piling up anxiety chemicals.

All threats to ourselves—whether psychological or physical, whether real or imagined—cause the production of real chemicals, which circulate throughout the body and the brain. These chemicals change the rate at which our lungs contract and our hearts pound while upping the tension in our "fight-or-flight" muscles, such as the arms, hips, back, and legs. These chemicals also cause mental changes: general anxiety and desire for fight and/or flight.

The purpose of defenses is to reduce or eliminate the feeling of threat. The less the feeling of threat, the less production of chemicals. The fewer fight-or-flight chemicals we produce the closer we are to approximating our range game.

Let's see how Insight-Oriented Defenses can make a surprising and immediate impact on our game.

SECTION 2: *Insight-Oriented Defenses Against Anxiety Chemicals: Defusing the Time Bomb*

Insight-Oriented Defenses

THESE DEFENSES are based on one simple but somewhat odd idea: that the reason why our range game breaks up on the course is hidden in our past.

Huh?

This is not an intuitive idea.

We're out here on the golf course. The sun is shining. We've just been crushing them on the range. But at some point on the course things go south.

But what has that got to do with the past? The past is dead, and isn't it only in science fiction and horror that the dead are able to come back to attack the living? Yeah, right.

Something is attacking the living. Hasn't everyone been astonished and mortified by a sudden blowout on the course? For some it's a complete surprise, and for others it's as if the undead had suddenly grabbed hold of the club. In all cases the swing feels different, and the results are appalling.

Being human, we are happily wedded to the idea of "cause and effect." We reason that there must be some *cause* for the bad drive. *Cause*, in our minds, is very close to *culprit*. Somebody has done something bad, and we want to know who.

After the bad drive, there is a moment when the fairway and the hazard that killed our effort become a crime scene. They might as well be marked off in yellow tape, with the ball and the divot outlined in chalk. Now we only have to round up the usual suspects.

We glare at people who are moving, we resent cheers and loud talk from neighboring greens. Wind and wet grass are eyed with suspicion. Maybe it's the new clubs we bought, or should have bought. This is the lineup of people or objects within earshot or eyesight. They certainly are all suspects.

Perhaps we say to ourselves, as if we were scolding someone else: "You really stink," or "Keep your head down," or "For once, would you just finish the swing?"

To the list of suspects (those who talked in our backswing, those who moved or who weren't in the right place, wind, and clubs) we sometimes add ourselves.

THE WHODUNIT

Someone has attempted to kill the ball. The rest of the foursome are attempting to recover the body (the ball). It's a crime scene, all right; and we find ourselves preoccupied with the question of who did it.

Sure, you swung the club; yet wouldn't it have gone straight but for the jubilant shouting on the next green? Or if Bill hadn't moved in your backswing? And how about the wind? And what about that lesson you took; hey, that could be part of the problem!

The bad shot-maker swears it will never happen again. But sometimes while still forswearing he begins swearing again: "Damn it, can't they keep it down? Hey! We're trying to play golf over here!"

You can continue to repeat this crime and punishment over and over. Bad shot? Ooh, that hurts! But hey, wait a minute: not my fault. Or the apparent opposite: Bad shot? Ooh, that hurts! But hey, wait a minute: entirely my fault. To the caddy or partner or pro: "I didn't keep my head down? I knew that." And then to yourself: "When are you going to learn to keep your head down?"

THE BLAME GAME

The Blame Game is what popular magazines would call it. Things go wrong, and we blame someone. The majority blame someone or something else. Yet there is a sizeable and vocal minority who blame themselves.

Those who blame themselves feel superior to those who blame outside influences.

Those who blame outside influences would feel even worse if they blamed themselves.

Who has the right take on this? Neither of the above. Most people sense this intuitively. Even if blaming someone else or oneself feels right initially, most people eventually experience a dead end with this mind-set. Nothing gets better. When the same problem recurs again and again, a reasonable person senses that there must be a better way to understand it.

THE RUSH TO JUDGMENT

Whenever there is an opportunity for blame, some will say someone else did it.

But perhaps we have achieved the next step in personal development, in which case we say, "It happened on my watch so I take full responsibility (although I don't seem to understand what happened)."

Now you may wonder at that last statement. The self-blamer ("Why can't you keep your head down?" et al.) sounds like he knows what is going on. But this is not the case. Because the same golf crime continues to be committed, over and over.

There is a need to get better. And there is a need to explain why one suddenly got worse. In the rock-paper-scissors game of golf the need to explain why one suddenly got worse usually covers the need to get better. Let's start there.

What is the rush to assign blame for a bad shot?

LONG AGO AND FAR, FAR AWAY

Long ago and far, far away we were children. Tennessee Williams said, "My father was a telephone line repairman who fell in love with long distances . . . he could have gone to the moon, but went much further—for time is the longest distance between two places."

Mr. Williams had a point. You can take the Concorde to England in three hours. You can fly tourist to Tokyo in 19 hours from New York. You—if you were an astronaut or had the wherewithal—could go to the moon in 97 hours.

But the past is much further away. We all know in fact that King Arthur and the ascension of Muhammad are inaccessible. Call any ticket agency: You can't get there from here.

The same is true of yesterday. Yesterday is as inaccessible as King Arthur's Court.

Surprisingly enough, the same is true of the first tee—if you are on the second hole (and even if you are on the first fairway). Every shot you have already made is as inaccessible as King Arthur's Court. It really doesn't matter when you stop to think about it. It could have happened two hundred million years ago, or two milliseconds ago. In any case, it is equally beyond your grasp. You can't change it.

Yet there is an overriding—almost an irresistible—urge to assign blame for the bad shot. When we think about it abstractly we can be quite philosophical. But on the course we practically have to bite our lips not to blurt some explanation of the bad shot, which, depending on our style, will implicate either ourselves or someone or something else.

ARE WE "ARRESTING" THE PROPER SUSPECTS?

When someone is arrested for a distinctive serial crime (the Son of Sam, the Night Stalker, etc.), there is one thing that we like to see. We like to see that crime stop.

If overly similar crimes continue to appear we start to wonder if we have the wrong bad guy in custody.

Of course, this is the problem with the blame game. The same golf crimes, the same hooks and slices and blades, continue to appear after we have blamed convenient others or our own intractable selves.

If the same crimes continue to appear we have to wonder if we have the right perps in custody. The self-blamers will have confessed, but what good is a confession if the criminal activity continues? If all the usual suspects, external and internal, have been detained and yet the criminal activity continues, then it must be time to examine other suspects.

THE WRONG MODEL

Actually, this is the wrong model. The idea of trying to find someone or something to blame for our psychological errors makes no more sense than trying to find someone or something to blame for our physical errors.

If we aren't the largest, strongest men and women we can blame our mothers: maybe they smoked cigarettes or drank alcohol, as people commonly did until recently. If we don't have natural swings grooved from an early age, maybe we should blame our fathers for not being golf pros, or our parents for not having joined country clubs when we were little.

Skipping over the absurdity of this approach, where is the efficacy? If the idea is to hit the ball farther, or straighter, or more consistently, will any amount of blaming help us attain that goal? Of course not.

We have some idea of where we want to go. But when we engage in the blame game we do nothing to advance ourselves in that direction. We become like the typical squabbling couple who have taken a wrong turn on a highway. He asks exasperatedly why she can't read a map. She is amazed that he didn't stop at that gas station twenty miles back to get directions like she told him to. The kids are screaming.

Is this getting them where they want to go quicker? No—just the opposite, of course. Now they are not only lost but they are also angry, and minutes and hours go by when they could have been getting on the right track. But they have something more important to do. They have to prove that it's not really their fault. The Blame Game takes its toll in life just as it does on the golf course.

We must exorcize the Blame Game; we need to uninstall it. It is not enough to promise ourselves we won't play the Blame Game. That's like promising yourself that you won't slice. If you don't know why you slice, then you will slice again no matter what you promise yourself or how sincere you are when you make that promise. If you don't know why you play the Blame Game, then you will play it again no matter how sincere you are when you swear you won't.

WHERE DID THE BLAME GAME COME FROM?

Let's imagine a little girl. Her name is Jane. She is three years old, playing with her favorite doll in the living room and drinking apple juice.

It's not that hard to imagine what happens next: the juice gets spilled on the rug.

Enter Mommy.

MOMMY: What happened here? (Pointing to juice stain)
JANE: Juice spill on rug, Mommy. Make big mess.

Jane says this very matter-of-fact, very like a three-year-old. If Mommy adds:

MOMMY: How did the juice spill, honey?
JANE: I spill it, Mommy.

Still very matter-of-fact, still with that inimitable three-year-old charm, which is how people sound before they have agendas. (Note how hard it is for anyone other than a trained actor or a great mimic to talk in the tone of a three-year-old. It's very hard for an adult to say something without another layer of messages being tacked on to the tone.)

One thing is clear as you listen to Jane: no Blame Game.

Now let's take a peek at Jane, age four. She is still in the living room, and the juice has just spilled.

MOMMY: What happened here? (Pointing to juice stain) How many times do I have to tell you not to drink juice in the living room!

Jane starts to cry, hugging her favorite doll, Raggedy Ann.

A year later Jane (now five) is again in the living room. The juice has just spilled.

MOMMY: What happened here?
JANE: I don't know.
MOMMY: That juice didn't spill itself. Who spilled it?
JANE: Raggedy Ann. She spilled the juice!
MOMMY: Jane, you are a very bad girl. Now go to your room.

Up in her room, a dry-eyed Jane turns to Raggedy Ann and says, "Raggedy Ann, you are a very bad girl. Now go to your room."

This is a key development. Jane has built the machinery inside her head, in the part we call the Upstairs, which will take on the role of the mother and the father in assigning blame and responsibility. She practices now on Raggedy Ann, but the machinery for assigning blame to the rest of her is coming into place. In computer language, she has written and installed a program on her hard drive that mimics and eventually replaces the outside policeman, the mother.

There are two great advantages for little Jane in this, which is why every one of us did the same thing when we were about this age, whether we remember it or not.

The first advantage is it keeps us out of trouble and pain. Nobody likes pain, and when Mommy says "Bad girl!" that is very painful to the small child. If the small child can anticipate being a bad girl and say to herself "Bad girl" as she is bringing juice into the living room, then her life becomes more pleasant. She is able to avoid actions that will provoke her own self-blame.

The second advantage is one of control. If Jane does in fact spill the juice, she can say "Bad girl" to herself. This is painful, but not as painful as having Mommy say it. Then if Mommy subsequently does say "Bad girl" to Jane, there is for Jane an element of "I knew that. I knew that already. No big deal."

For an adult on the golf course, this translates into "I didn't keep my head down? I knew that."

By the age of six Jane doesn't need Johnnie Cochran.

MOMMY:	What happened here?
JANE:	Mikey (her little brother) spilled it. (Or Rover the dog knocked it over, or it was already spilled when she came into the living room.)
MIKEY:	It was Jane, Mommy.
JANE:	No, it wasn't!
MIKEY:	Yes, it was!
MOMMY (EXASPERATED):	I don't care who did it. You both help clean it up, right now!

For an adult on the golf course, this translates into "They were talking in my backswing" (they did it), or "The caddie misclubbed me" (he did it), or "Can't even get a level lie in the tee box!" (the greenskeeper did it).

PROFIT-AND-LOSS STATEMENT FOR THE BLAME GAME

It's actually easier to see what we give up with the Blame Game than it is to see what we get.

The Blame Game only occurs after something has gone wrong. We give up two things. First, we give up our equanimity. We give up our calm. Whenever we blame we are angry. Anger sends a message to the chemical factory to make fight chemicals. Sure, we know there is no need to make fight chemicals, but in the factory they just do what they are told. The chemical factory has no eyes and no ears, it simply gets E-mail from the primitive brain. Anger means angry chemicals. These tighten our muscles, as we have seen, as well as cause other subtle physiological changes—which would all be good if we were about to fight a saber-toothed tiger, but which make it harder to hit a golf ball well.

And if, with all these chemicals around, we then hit another golf ball not well (the modern equivalent of again spilling the fruit juice), then there will be more blaming and more chemicals. This is one reason why bad shots, like black widows, come in pairs—sometimes even in bunches.

Second, we give up a timely opportunity to figure out what is going wrong, to right the ship before it takes on more water. Right after the shot our impressions are fresh. At that point a calm curiosity about what went wrong—because something certainly went wrong— may yield results. By the time we are done blaming others or ourselves, the actual event, the tiny physical impressions we are able to retain of a swing that only lasted fractions of a second, is something of a blur. We remember the result, but the process is obscured. The ground has been trampled by our own inner detectives and prosecutors, and whatever small footprints or other clues may have been available are now lost forever. And to make matters more frustrating, they are lost forever over and over!

Unfortunately, we are like the couple who made the wrong turn in the car. Arguing about whose fault it was rather than trying to figure out where one went wrong is particularly damaging if you take this same road every day. We will continue to make the same wrong turn over and over and never seriously go back and look at why that happens and how we could avoid that if we are preoccupied by the Blame Game.

Okay. That is what we give up. Certainly it is a lot. Do we get anything in return?

You can be sure that we get plenty in return; in fact, you can be sure that we get back more than we give up or we wouldn't do it.

The mind is trying to look out for us, and whatever way we are doing things is the best way for us. From the mind's point of view.

That is why it is so hard to change the way we are doing things—because the mind thinks that on balance however we are doing things is the best way to do them. We didn't start out doing things the way we do them right now; over many years, our current mode of operations emerged as the best and safest way to get as much as possible of what we want while getting as little as possible of what we don't want.

The problem is that the values the mind is working with are not in today's numbers. So when the mind solves the equations it is using archaic values; it gets what seem to be odd or wrong answers. But the answers are right given the data the mind is working with.

It is no good to tell the mind to do something different. The mind wants to do what is best for you; but extremely important parts of the mind (the Upstairs, for example) are quite used to the idea that you do not know what is good for you. You are the spiller of fruit juice on the carpet, and you are the one who is miserable when Mommy yells. Sure, you want juice, but the mind knows better.

And at a time when drinking juice in the living room was worth, let's say, a plus one on the pleasure scale, and a scolding from Mommy was worth a minus five on the pleasure scale, the mind was right. You might have wanted to take that juice back to the living room, but the mind saw the folly of that. And after you spilled the juice, if Mommy scolded you it was minus five—but if you scolded yourself it was minus four, and if you were able to somehow realize that it was really Mikey or the dog's fault, then it was only minus two. So the mind is looking out for you, when it finds someone else to blame. But perhaps you are thinking that the juice was spilled long ago.

The problem is that there is no sense of time in the Upstairs, and the Upstairs still thinks that a scolding from Mommy is minus five on the pleasure scale.

And the Upstairs has made the modern translation. It's not worried just about fruit juice and rugs. Anything you are not supposed to do will lead to a scolding from Mommy, or—courtesy of the program you wrote for yourself when you were young—a scolding from yourself. But the scolding we give ourselves ("Bad girl!") has some of the force of a scolding from Mommy, and can make us feel almost as bad. Not completely as bad, or the economies would not be there for us to replace Mommy's scolding with our own. But if our scolding makes us feel minus four on the pleasure scale instead of minus five, that is still plenty bad.

Our mind is using an old value of minus four for our "clumsy" errors, and this is a lot of pain.

Every child learned to blame and to some extent "believe" that Raggedy Ann or Mikey or the dog did it, because that made the pain less (minus two). With these values in place the mind tries to find someone else to blame when we hit a bad shot, or to blame ourselves before someone else can, in order to protect us from internal pain.

You cannot talk the mind out of this process; the mind will protect you whether you ask it to or not. This part of the mind is a primitive organ designed to protect us in spite of ourselves. You can command your heart to stop beating, but it won't do it. The heart is another primitive organ designed to protect us by acting whether we want it to or not.

We can control the heart by changing the data that it has to work with, however. If we thin out the oxygen in the air, it will beat faster to make up for this. If we don't drink any water so that our blood volume goes down, the heart will beat harder and faster to make up for it. If we drink lots and lots of water the heart will read the data and slow down again.

In a similar fashion we cannot simply tell the Upstairs not to bother with assigning blame. But we can change the values that it receives and thus alter its response.

WINNING THE BLAME GAME

It almost seems as though, as the giant computer says in the movie *WarGames*, "the only winning move is not to play." But there is another winning move, and it is available to us.

The other winning move is to change the values that the primitive Upstairs brain is working with. Change the scoring of "Bad Shot" from minus four to minus three and life is measurably better. But why stop there? Change it to minus one, and there is so little pain there is no need to deflect any of it onto others.

Change it to zero for best results. Neutral is the desired response. This unleashes our natural ally, curiosity.

We all start out curious, but blame and shame distract us from our natural state. The three-year-old Jane is curious about the way the apple juice makes the interesting mark on the rug. She might even try pouring it out again, and again, until she gets the hang of how it works, then move on to something else.

We really need to take *good* and *bad* out of our thinking, because we want to get away from the idea that we did something bad (which starts the whole Blame Game cycle). Mortification and embarrassment and shame and humiliation are the true underlying emotions of the (psychologically) average golfer after hitting a "bad" shot in public. These are also the responses of children scolded or ridiculed for things they know they shouldn't have done.

To change the value setting on the "bad" shot, we must reframe it as the "unexpected" shot. We must think of ourselves not as small children hiding inside of large bodies desperately trying not to make a mistake and be found out; we must think of ourselves as some kind of curious predictor of events. We estimate that the upcoming collision between a club head moving at 90 miles per hour, more or less, and a small ball of 1⅝-inch diameter will result in this or that trajectory or distance. Usually we can expect to be surprised, sometimes by the very unexpected. But since we are a self-correcting computer, since we are "students of the game," we can reasonably and curiously wonder how it came to pass that a particular ball took such a surprising turn!

And there is always a reason. The club face was open and the ball, of course, flew out to the right (worth remembering in case you ever want to do that on purpose). Then file it away and move on to the next prediction. Depending on your handicap, you can reasonably expect to be surprised on a golf course some predictable number of times per round. On a low-scoring day, you will be surprised somewhat less often.

The great Bobby Jones said that in an 18 hole round no more than six or seven shots went as he had anticipated. That he said this shows he had intuitively arrived at what this chapter makes explicit for you to appropriate into your own game.

We can only formulate guesses as to what will happen when the club head hits the ball, and if Bobby Jones was surprised most of the time, then we should look forward to being surprised, too.

Of course, we can look at what caused the surprise result. If it is a pleasant surprise, naturally we'll want to leave that ingredient in; if it is an unpleasant surprise, we will want to remove or modify the suspect ingredient. This will make our predictions that much more accurate.

And so we go around the course with plenty to surprise and sometimes delight us, not least of which is the absence of that tedious Blame Game. "Gee, I wonder why that happened" is good. "Whose fault was that?" is, well, bad.

Uninstalling the Blame Game

It would be nice if we could just click "uninstall" and the Blame Game would evaporate. But even on a computer, uninstalling a program isn't always that easy. And the truth is that we need some of the structures that are intimately involved in the Blame Game: ethics, morals, everything we "should" or "ought" to do comes from the same structure. Our sense of personal responsibility would be wholly absent without the Upstairs. So what we are doing is something much more subtle than uninstalling the Upstairs. We are simply revising the rules, resetting the values, which the Upstairs uses to calculate what will work out best for us.

Specifically, we are taking the errant shot out of the category of fruit juice spilled on a rug—the category of things we know (because how many times have we been told?) we should not do but willfully do anyway.

Now when you look at it like that, it makes sense. That is the wrong category for the errant shot. The little girl wants to drink juice in the living room on the rug, despite the fact—or because of it—she was told not to. An arbitrary authority, but one with the power to make you feel bad, tells you not to do something yet you want to do it anyway. As adults we have many things that fall into that category also: everything from double parking to adultery, from an extra "sick day" at work to deducting a nonbusiness lunch. Some or all of these are typical of things that for a fleeting moment tempt many. You know you shouldn't, you know a powerful force may make you feel bad; and often you intervene in advance to make yourself feel bad or to warn yourself away. This is the proper business of the Upstairs.

But how did the errant golf shot get into this category, anyway? Even if the bad news is "that's the hanging judge," the good news is that "we're in the wrong courtroom."

We don't know that it is "wrong" to hit the errant shot, and in any case we certainly are not tempted to hit the errant shot. There is a court in the Upstairs that punishes us when we deliberately do what we know to be wrong or forbidden, and we've been trying ourselves in that court every time we hit a "bad" shot. We need a change of venue.

This would be the situation in which it would be appropriate for the Upstairs to scold us, as it has been doing: If we were playing golf on a resort course lined with condos and expensive houses; and if for some reason we were tempted to tee one up and bang it off a condo roof; and if someone kept saying, "Hey, don't do that, how many times have I told you not to do that?"; and if we then teed up anyway and gave it a whack right at the nearest roof—well, that would be like Jane and the puddle of juice. Then we could attack ourselves for doing the wrong thing: "Bad Jane!" And then we could look around for any excuse: "I didn't do it, he did it!" or "The wind must have taken it," or "Damn, I picked my head up again," or "The caddie gave me the wrong club!" But until that time the Blame Game is misplaced.

We are not in the situation for which the Blame Game was devised, so it is inappropriate to employ it.

How do we come to make this mistake in the first place? This is a very good question. What tricked us into associating what happens when we hit an errant shot with what happened when we did what we were not supposed to do when we were young? This is puzzling until we step back a little.

Hey! You know what? We don't always make this mistake.

On the range we hit errant shots, but we don't go ballistic. In fact, on the range we are much more the way we are supposed to be: curious about the reason a ball went astray; changing this or that; fulfilling our prediction of a good shot more often. When you stop to think about it, the Blame Game pops up only on the course, and particularly in the presence of others.

The key words are not "bad shot," after all! It is not the bad (or errant) shot that triggers the "Bad Jane" response. It is *the presence of others*. In the presence of others we revert to a situation where we could have done what pleased, but did not. At that time it was less painful, as we have seen, to blame someone else, or to beat Mommy to the punch in blaming ourselves. The presence of others triggers this early and formerly effective defense.

But however effective this defense against pain was formerly, it is misplaced now and causes more pain than it alleviates.

In the presence of others we look down and see a "mess." By reflex this activates our ingrained childhood response when a parent caught us after the juice was spilled. We immediately start with either "I didn't do it, it was his/her/its fault!" or "Bad Me!" or "Darn! How could you spill that?"

That this is triggered not by bad shots but rather by the presence of others helps explain one of the things that puzzles and frustrates you and almost everybody else. Why is your range game better than your course game? Well, as we have seen, this primitive saga of crime and punishment that culminates in the Blame Game is activated on the course but not on the range by the presence of observers. We attribute to them the disapproval we reflexively expect from others when we make mistakes. Then the defense we marshal against this anticipated disapproval snowballs into a force that ironically further detracts from our shot-making ability, leading to a vicious cycle of further anticipated blame and further poor results.

Eliminate the Blame Game and you have taken one important step toward restoring your range game to the course.

IT TAKES A "MENTAL SWING CHANGE" TO REMOVE THE BLAME GAME

Surprisingly enough, you need to reread or think through this section a few times until it becomes "second nature."

Although, if this were a physical swing change, the parallel pre-scription would not be surprising. It is common with a swing change—new grip, a move further to the inside, larger hip shift, etc.—to practice the new motion for many swings a day in front of a mirror at home. And it is generally accepted that the new swing will not be "ingrained in muscle memory" for several weeks.

Why should it be surprising, then, to find that you have to "repeat" a series of "new thoughts" before they will become ingrained enough to be more natural than the old thoughts, particularly when the old thoughts represent the way we have been thinking ever since we were children?

Intuitively, we feel that if we read something and it makes sense, or if we decide to think in a particular way, then we will be immediately able to do that.

Well, when we first took up golf we probably assumed that someone could show us how to do something with the club and that we would just be able to do it. It is only through experience that we have learned how hard it is to truly incorporate even a small change into our game.

The same is true of a mental change. But when you have thought often enough about "Jane"—and how she constructed an "Upstairs" in her head to warn and punish herself—you will have carved out a different pathway of thought inside *your* head. If you reflect repeatedly on similar processes that took place in your life, you will succeed in rewriting your own program and eliminating the Blame Game. Since this way of thinking is more accurate, more efficient, causes you less pain, and gains you more rewards, it will succeed in replacing the old way of thinking. But that won't happen overnight, and like any physical change it will require repetition. Reading passages out loud or before you go to sleep, or recording them on a cassette and playing them back through headsets on the way to work may speed the process. Or simply thinking it through may work for you. Anything that allows *curiosity* to replace *blame* will work, and will work wonders!

And it should be noted that mental changes are like physical changes in another way as well. A physical swing change requires repetition before it becomes natural; but even after it seems natural in a pressureless (range) situation, it still will not be as strong under pressure as the rest of your game. For the physical change to become habitual even under pressure only comes after prolonged use. This is true in all sports; tennis fans can think of Steffi Graf's topspin backhand as a good example. She needed to develop that shot to beat Gabriela Sabatini. As a late acquisition it was, for a long time, more fragile than the rest of her game, and in fact never became 100 percent reliable under pressure.

The same is true of a mental change; the greater the pressure the more likely we are to revert to the old way of thinking. The point here is that even if you decrease your blaming behavior and increase your enjoyment and your progress at the same time, you may still find yourself reverting to your old ways at some point. The key is not to be too discouraged by this, not to begin blaming yourself for blaming yourself. It is better at that point to patiently reread or rethink this chapter, and to accept the fact that all changes—physical and mental—take time to harden into the truly durable.

But eventually they do. Everything we do flawlessly now was once new. Once upon a time we all had to sound out words as we attempted to read. Yet you're not worried that you will have any trouble with the next sentence. Soon you won't be giving a thought to having any trouble with the next shot.

CAN'T GIVE UP THE BLAME GAME?

Many players can benefit greatly or completely from the preceding section. Some won't.

Those who relate to the preceding section but find themselves still playing the Blame Game should read this section, which explains the underlying theory and proceeds beyond it.

TOO ANGRY AT PARENTS TO GIVE UP THE BLAME GAME

Giving up the Blame Game is based upon the insight that you are not fundamentally angry at the people who move during your swing, or the people who shouted during your swing, or whatever. The idea is that your parents judged you when you were little and made you feel bad when you didn't do well.

Now, in the present, when you don't do well you anticipate your parents' criticism. And to shortcut that mortifying experience, you are searching for something to be mad at to deflect your parents' anger.

The treatment outlined is basically to make you aware that you are angry at your parents. It will not work in all cases. It will not work if you can say, "So? Why shouldn't I blame my parents? I'm still mad at my parents."

People who think this way remain angry at their parents, and their parents' surrogates—the other golfers, the wind, the sand trap. All obstacles on the course continue to represent the parent, and the anger is unresolved. To avoid having this continue to retard golf improvement, one must resolve the anger at the parent.

This exercise is simple, but difficult. The difficult part is that people feel they are giving up something when they give up being angry at their parents. So they are reluctant to do so. The simple part is that, as Yeats says, when they have done so, "so great a sweetness flows."

You only have to realize that your parents, however wrong-headed and malignant, were doing the best they could. Hard to believe.

Yeah, okay, it was bad. But consider them, consider their nature and circumstances. That's all they had to offer, that was the best they could do. If they could have done better, they would have. They didn't; they couldn't.

When we take things personally, when we feel they were aimed in particular at us, we take them badly.

A golf example is helpful. If we are being held up by a slow foursome and the people behind us deliberately hit balls that roll around our feet, won't we be outraged? But if a doddering old man on the next fairway slices a ball that rolls near our golf cart we are not overly perturbed.

In our assessment of whether or not to get angry we take into account *intention*.

If people intended to make us feel bad, we are more inclined to be angry at them.

Those who are angry with their parents feel on some level that their parents deliberately make them feel bad. They feel their parents deliberately "hit at" them.

The key to making peace with our parents (and with our golf game) is the realization that they couldn't do any better. Our parents were more like the dodderer from the other fairway who sent the ball around our ankles by accident.

Every son or daughter harbors to a greater or lesser degree the fantasy that their parents could change, could be "better" parents. (Many are locked in a struggle predicated upon the idea that because of that selfsame struggle, the parents will see the light and suddenly become "better" parents.) They appear to be struggling, but they are really waiting—waiting for their parents to see the light.

These well-meaning sons and daughters wait in vain. Parents will not change. The only item in the equation that can change is the expectation of the child.

When we give up on our parents, our golf game improves. When we truly realize that our parents did the best they could, however pathetic that best was, that is when we stop blaming them. When we stop blaming our parents (which we didn't even know we were doing), that is when we stop blaming their surrogates, their stalking-horses, their substitutes. That is when we stop blaming the wind and the water, the movers and the shouters. That is when we stop blaming everything in the here and now that seems to annoy us simply because it represents everything in there and then that does actually still annoy us.

That is when our mental handicap improves.

SIBLING RIVALRY

The exercises in Chapter 2 may not work for a special case of the undead, of the past attacking the present—where the unresolved feelings relate to a brother or a sister, rather than to a parent.

The appearance of the golf difficulty is different in this situation. In the sibling rivalry situation, the difficulty is triggered by play with particular types of individuals. Specifically, those who are psychologically reminiscent of the brother or sister can invoke the curse. Usually, this is an older brother or sister, and often the activated feelings are those of extreme competitiveness, or its opposite.

YOU SEEM TO STOP TRYING . . .

A man who was meek and quiet because that was the only way to get his older brother to stop picking on him may later become meek and quiet in the presence of an aggressive older sibling equivalent—a boss or a person of higher rank in a similar line of work, often only slightly older.

The player may find himself "letting" the opponent win. At an earlier age the player usually found that little resistance was the best way to get the bullying to stop. Now the thoughtful player is wondering why in certain situations he seems to "give up." Antidote: The older brother or sister clearly had problems of their own. The bullying had little or nothing to do with who you were. You could have been anybody, anybody you know and anybody you could shake a stick at, and the result would have been the same. That is to say any younger brother or sister would have sufficed as a target: Being a target had nothing to do with you in particular. They would have picked on anybody who was smaller and who was there. You were just in the wrong place at the wrong time, that's all.

As long as you think what most people in this situation think— that the attack had something to do with you and, specifically, that you could have done something to prevent it—then you will continue to be stuck in the ancient solution of passivity, of letting the other guy win. The unconscious feeling is that what worked before will work again. The unconscious corollary is that you are the kind of person who is picked on by certain types, and that the only safe thing is to offer little resistance.

But look around. Does this look like the home you grew up in? Do these bully players look like your brother or sister?

And most important, being passive, letting them win, had nothing to do with it. If they had the interest or the nerve, they would have continued tormenting you anyway. They stopped for the same reason they started, because of problems of their own. You are free now. Use your freedom to beat some lesser players.

And remember what we said before. The past is far away. Your school days are as far away as King Arthur's Court. No one from those days can harm you now, unless you conjure them up in your imagination. But why would you do that? You wouldn't, because a bully is well-placed when sealed into the past. The best revenge against people who bullied us in our past is to ignore them.

You won't conjure up a tormentor from the past because you would rather win in the present. And when you open your eyes, there is no one from the past. There are only people from the present. When you open your eyes and look around you, there is no visible reason not to play your best and have a good time.

4

You Are Desperate to Win, but Can't

YOU SEEM TO TRY TOO HARD . . .

The sibling rivalry problem often evokes the opposite reaction. When playing with certain types of players you become angry, desperate to win. You try too hard. You swing too hard, your muscles are too tight. You want to win so bad you can't.

This is more like the saber-toothed tiger reaction, activated by a player who reminds you psychologically of the brother or sister (or parent or classmate) you were competitive with a long time ago. But in this case, rather than roll over and play dead, you reacted with good old caveman rage.

Now in certain situations you are still reacting with controlled rage. People who have this reaction will recognize it. In the present, it manifests as certain players you really want to beat or a certain player who is annoying and who you hate to play, but, when you do, you find yourself overly concerned with winning, more than usually interested in their hitting a bad shot, and hoping their game will fall apart almost as much as or more than you are hoping your game will come together.

Often these people are themselves overly competitive. They may be acting out their own sibling rivalry, which is what unconsciously triggers yours. They are treating you like a disliked sibling, which in turn reminds you of how your absent sibling treated you, and you begin to treat them the way you used to treat your own sibling.

To the outside observer there are two golfers now strolling around a beautiful golf course on a sunny day. But this is far from what is happening on the inside. On the inside a two-person play is being performed. And what typecasting! For the role of angry sibling number one we have found an annoying golfer who, underneath a smiling exterior, still harbors an unresolved desire to best his "brother." And for the role of brother number two we have found the perfect actor: you. Since the desire not to be beaten by your fiercely competitive brother still burns brightly somewhere inside you, you are perfect in the role of the other brother who won't give in, who gives as good as he gets, who isn't going to take it anymore.

There are two problems with this "play." It isn't conducive to good golf and it isn't fun (for you). As an angry brother, your muscles are too tight to play well, and your other caveman responses (see Caveman) are also interfering with your performance. The worse you play, the more angry and frustrated you become, because playing badly and losing are hard enough to deal with, but they are particularly humiliating and frustrating when you are locked in a struggle with your long-lost brother.

ANTIDOTE

To understand the antidote we must first answer an important question. The question is, why are you losing anyway? Isn't he struggling with the same sibling problem that you are? Is it affecting you more than it is affecting him?

The answer is yes. It is affecting you more than it is affecting him, and that is precisely why you are losing. He is more comfortable with this situation than you are. He goes around all the time looking for a sibling substitute to beat. Not just on the golf course either. Work, home life, on the road, everywhere, he is looking for a sibling substitute to beat.

If you think this can't be much fun, you're right. And certainly it's not that much fun for those who are around him. Which is why you are better liked than he is, and which is why in general you enjoy life more than he does. Unfortunately, this specific arena—the reenactment of bitter childhood competition—is the only situation where he has more fun than you do.

Of course, this is relative. Look at him: He is not having all that much fun either. But he is like a pit bull who has sunk his teeth into another dog though he himself is being bitten at the same time. It's not fun, exactly, but it is what he does. The fight-or-flight caveman chemicals aren't helping his game either, but he is more used to their presence. His game is built on the premise that these chemicals will be present, while yours is built on the premise that they will be absent.

A good game without these chemicals is better than a good game with these chemicals. That is why you are a better golfer than he is (on the range). That is also why you are a better golfer than he is when you aren't playing against him (when the caveman chemicals aren't infecting your swing). Unfortunately, in the situation where you both have caveman chemicals he is a better golfer than you are. And that is the situation you are permitting to happen every time you play against him.

It would be easy to say that all you have to do is resolve this lingering anger at your sibling. However, that could take awhile, and this book is about getting better now, or at least soon. Fortunately, it isn't necessary to use a jackhammer to kill a fruit fly. We can get out of this bind more simply than that.

We don't really have to get rid of sibling rivalry to play good golf. We simply have to understand and accept it. Hidden agendas are what disrupt our game. You are walking around with a desire to push back at someone who wants to push you; that is why you are a sucker for his act. Harsh words, but the truth, and, at least in this case, the truth will make you free. You are not comfortable with the idea that you contain within you an angry cavechild who is still looking to assert himself. But you must, since you get drawn into an overly competitive stance in the presence of an overly competitive golfer.

Just because a part of you wants to do something doesn't mean you have to do it. Everyone has small temptations that are ignored every day. Similarly, we can ignore the temptation to get into a "pissing contest"[1] with the aggressive golfer. It is just that in order to ignore the temptation we have to be aware of it first. When we aren't aware of it, we just give in to it. We start reenacting the sibling situation without even being consciously aware of what we are doing.

We are giving in to a temptation in the same mindless way we might eat the whole can of cashews or the entire carton of ice cream. Afterward, we may be more or less miserable, but in some way some part of us wanted to do it in the first place. When we are aware of the temptation, we can pass up the unhealthy snack.

All right, you say. You get it. The idea is simply not to have these feelings when the aggressive golfer is present. But isn't that harder than it sounds? Isn't the whole point that the aggressive golfer activates these dormant feelings, awakens the sleeping caveman, as it were?

Yes, it is true that you and the aggressive golfer have "chemistry." Unlike the "chemistry" that young men and women describe on first dates, this is bad chemistry, unpleasant chemistry, but chemistry nonetheless.

---

[1]This common and vulgar expression reflects the fact that men are more easily sidetracked into this sort of "who is more macho" dead end. Nonetheless, many women will also recognize these dynamics.

The first key to breaking the cycle is in viewing the aggressive golfer differently. Don't use your gut, use your head. See that golfer not as one individual, but as an individual desperately looking for someone else to butt heads with.

The next key is to use the aggression this naturally triggers in you, rather than trying to ignore it (see Swing Thoughts for more on the importance of utilizing aggression rather than simply trying to pretend that it doesn't exist). Imagine this guy bucking his head ludicrously like a bull or a ram or a goat, desperately searching for somebody to lock horns with.

Now, what punishes this guy more, butting heads with him or watching him run around butting the air as he gets more and more desperate to play his favorite game? His favorite game, of course, isn't golf—it's butting heads.

He will try to needle you, annoy you, whatever it takes to get you going. Since you see what he is up to you can further frustrate him by not engaging.

It takes some practice at ignoring the urge to butt heads before it withers away, but wither away it will. And fortunately there are plenty of these head-butters on every golf course for you to practice on. When the aggressive golfer is paired with you, you will no longer think "Oh, no" or "I'm going to get him this time." Instead, you will think "Great. Here is a chance to practice the mental game of ignoring the head-butter, which will frustrate him, and will help lower my mental handicap." From the mental point of view, going up against the aggressive golfer is like having a chance to master an unusual hole or a different and challenging course.

And eventually you will regard the aggressive golfer in a similar fashion—as part of the course. He is like a sand trap. You appreciate the point of them, because otherwise the course would be too easy, like a sod farm. But just because you appreciate the point of a sand trap doesn't mean you want to get involved with it. And, as with a sand trap, the better you are at dealing with it the less you have to fear it. Less fear chemicals—less fight-or-flight chemicals—means more range game.

SECTION 3: *Other Mental Defenses Against Anxiety Chemicals*

5

Cognitive Defenses

IN THE last chapter, we saw how the past is crouching, ready to jump out into the present to eat our golf game for lunch.

We saw how blaming behavior, and how both increased passivity and increased aggressiveness—all interfering with our golf game—apparently were generated by present circumstances but actually were outgrowths of past unresolved conflict.

In this chapter, we will see an entirely different view of the mental problems that attack our golf game, and we will learn an alternative method for quieting the chemicals.

In the mental golf world, as in the physical golf world, there is more than one way to skin a cat.

If you are slicing, your pro may change your grip. He may work with your release, try to adjust your swing plane, or fine-tune your take-away.

The same is true of the mental game. If your mental handicap needs to be lowered, there is more than one way to go about doing that.

Insight-oriented defenses, as we have seen, are based on the idea that we have unresolved conflicts from the past that are activated in the present.

A relatively modern and extremely interesting theory maintains an almost opposite point of view. The cognitive view is as follows:

There is a superabundance of information available to us. We are like computers facing an overflow of input. If we tried to process all the information, we would be overwhelmed. In order to function, we allow a fraction of the total amount of information to filter through for forwarding to our internal computer. Clearly, the selection process of this information influences our sense of what is going on around us.

Furthermore, when information reaches us we make almost instantaneous value judgments about that information. Those values are transmitted to our internal chemical factory, and the chemicals appropriate to them are produced.

These instantaneous value judgments (called "automatic thoughts" by Aaron Beck and his followers who have popularized this theory) are often not reasonable. But because they are produced so quickly, they are not subjected to the usual scrutiny of the Ground Floor (see How the Mind Works), which applies logic to our experiences. As a consequence, we have unreasonable thoughts eliciting real, painfully real, physical responses from our body. These physical responses attack our range game, bringing it down to the level of our course game. Simply by correcting the Flash-Golf-Thoughts, by making them reasonable rather than unreasonable, we reduce the chemicals produced by the original unreasonable thought. Less chemicals means more range game.

The treatment consists of two parts. First you have to identify your Flash-Golf-Thoughts. Then you have to correct those which are unreasonable.

How it works

Take a situation that normally bothers you. This could be the first tee, or hitting over sand to the green, or hitting over water, or playing through another group, or playing up 18 with the clubhouse crowd watching, as well as any number of other situations. For this example, we will use hitting over water.

Nancy is a talented golfer, though she doesn't play as often as she would like. She has a part-time job and two children, so time is limited.

There is a very nice municipal course near her house where she sometimes plays when the kids are in school. The par 5 thirteenth requires her to lay up in front of the pond after her second shot. Then she has a 75-yard wedge over water to the green.

This is a shot she makes repeatedly on the range, but she dreads this hole on the course. In taking a history of her concern, we find that this hole did not bother her when she first began playing this course. At first she does not remember when this hole started to be a problem, but then recalls that several years ago in an important match she topped one directly into the pond. She is not sure whether it started then or not, but in any case over the last year her anxiety at the third shot on this hole has mounted. Sometimes even on the green of the preceding 12th hole, Nancy is already anticipating this water shot. Of course, that isn't doing much for her putting on the 12th hole either. So there is even more riding on fixing this.

We ask her to bring a piece of paper and a pencil with her to the course the next time she plays. She can use the score card if she likes. We ask her to write down immediately after the shot the thoughts that went through her head just before or during her swing. This is a difficult assignment. These flash-thoughts are practically subliminal: They appear on our mental screen long enough for our unconscious mind to apprehend them, but barely long enough for us to notice that any thought took place.

Some people think visually, and some think verbally. For the verbally inclined, these are mumbled mutterings at a very busy time, and we have to strain to hear them. Especially since these thoughts are transmitted at E-mail speed to our internal chemical factory just in time to squirt the chemicals that tighten our muscles just enough to spoil our shot—so that we are preoccupied by the subsequent "Oh, no!," which drowns out the original message.

After Nancy has played the hole several times, paying more and more attention to her internal flash-thoughts that immediately precede or accompany her shot over water on the 13th, she returns to us with two phrases scribbled on the back of a scorecard.

> I'm going to hit it into the water again.
> I'm going to top it.

We ask her a difficult question. We ask her—on a scale of 0 to 100, with 100 being absolutely certain—how certain is she at the precise moment that she has the thought "I'm going to hit it into water" that she is in fact going to hit it into the water? Does she think that the ball is absolutely going to go into the water (100)? Or that it couldn't possibly go into the water (0)? Or somewhere in between? What is her expectation at that precise moment as the club head is descending toward the ball?

She says that in all honesty it is about 80.

We ask her about her expectation that she is going to top it, and she assigns this about a 65.

We then ask her the corollary question: At that point when you estimate you have an 80 percent chance of hitting the ball into the water, or a 65 percent chance of topping it, how anxious on a scale of 0 to 100 are you, with 100 being the most anxious you have ever been? She answers 90.

Well, 70 to 100 is typical; but 70 to 100 is also pretty anxious. Ninety is certainly very anxious.

You have a chemical factory deep inside your body. You could liken this to America's nuclear defense command center, buried deep within the earth. Down there they don't see anything of what is actually going on up here. Deep in the command center they only respond to the signals that are transmitted to them from the "eyes and ears," from lookout centers up here on the surface. If the message transmitted is "danger" they prepare to launch. If the message is "we are under attack," then they release what to them is an appropriate response.

The same is true for your body. Deep inside you have a Command Center. It is prepared to launch fight-or-flight chemicals if you are under attack. You inherited this Command Center. Since the time of the caveman, this Command Center has been inside of us. When the saber-toothed tiger appears, the Command Center gets the message "saber-toothed tiger!" Immediately, the chemicals are launched, and in a fraction of a second they strike their many targets; the muscles, the heart rate regulator, the breathing regulator, the anxiety center.

This is a neat system, for a caveman. If you want to take a club and hit a saber-toothed tiger on the head so hard that it lies down, these are useful chemicals. If you want to run back to the cave faster than you have ever run before, these are useful chemicals.

If you want to hit a wedge seventy-five yards, these are not useful chemicals. In fact, they are poison.

Now we ask Nancy to assign a probability to the flash-thoughts that pop into her mind as she is about to hit over water. Nancy ponders the thought:

I'm going to hit it into the water again.

We ask her to assign a probability to that thought. At that moment how likely is it that she will hit this 75-yard shot into the water?

She says, "Well, of course, I won't do that. That is a shot I can easily make."

We point out to her what is one of the most important ingredients of this treatment. It must be accurate. It certainly isn't true that she can make this shot 100 percent of the time (if that were true, we would never have met her).

It is very important to remove the Pollyanna from our thinking. Friends and family may tell you that you can make this shot for sure. This will not help you, because on some level you know that this is not a true statement.

What is important is that you assign, to the best of your ability, a truly accurate probability to the shot.

We discuss this with Nancy. We ask her, "Realistically, and be 100 percent honest—don't overstate it (empty bragging), and don't understate it (false modesty)—if you have this shot to make one hundred times, how often do you make it?"

She hesitates. We prompt, "Ten percent? Ninety percent? What's your gut take, without thinking? Seventy-five yards, over water. How often do you make this shot?"

Nancy contemplates for a moment, then answers, "Ninety percent."

We reply, "Fine." She hastens to add, "But that still means that I miss it ten percent of the time."

We ask her, "Suppose that you are facing a shot that you know you miss ten percent of the time. How anxious are you?"

She thinks a little while, because she is a serious person, and responds, "I am vaguely anxious, or perhaps not at all."

We point out to her that she has assigned a 10 percent probability to hitting the ball into the water on the 13th hole, so why is she 70 to 100 percent anxious over a 10 percent probability?

She thinks carefully about this, nods, and says, "If I have a ten percent chance of messing up the shot, I should be about ten percent anxious."

And, on follow-up, her anxiety had practically disappeared on the 13th hole, which she had renamed Lucky 13 instead of Unlucky 13, as she had always thought of it before.

You need to contemplate honestly a situation that evokes anxiety in you. You must ask yourself these two questions:

What do I assume (honestly) is the percentage chance things will go wrong as I am about to hit the shot? (For this example assume the answer is 80.)

What do I estimate (honestly) as the actual chance that things will go wrong on this particular shot? (For this example assume the answer is 25.)

Then you ask yourself, "How anxious am I when I feel I have an 80 percent chance of failing?" On a scale of 0 to 100 the answer is _____. (For this example we will assume the answer is 80.)

Finally, you ask yourself, "How anxious am I when I feel I have a 25 percent chance of failing?" On a scale of 0 to 100 the answer is _____. (For this example we will assume the answer is 30.)

Since you estimate a 25 percent chance of failing in this particular shot (over water, let us say), then it must be appropriate to contemplate it with the anxiety that you would assign to a shot with that degree of risk, which is 30.

Reread this section until the math makes sense. This is a treatment that works relatively better, in our experience, with those who prefer a "logical" approach, but it can help anyone who assigns an inappropriate degree of anxiety to any given shot or situation.

LAND MINE THOUGHTS

There are certain thoughts that, if you happen to trip over them, will blow up your golf game. Many golfers who have high mental handicaps subscribe to one or more of these incorrect golf thoughts.

1. "IF I DON'T HIT IT WELL OFF THE FIRST TEE, I WON'T HAVE A GOOD ROUND."

This is a thought that adds extra pressure to an already pressure-filled moment (see First Tee Anxiety, Chapter 20) and has no basis in fact. In any round there are a number of good tee shots, a number of mediocre tee shots, and a number of bad tee shots. It doesn't matter what the order is. You could crack it off the first, and slice it off the eighteenth. Conversely, you could slice it off the first and crack it on some other hole.

The lower your handicap, the lower the number of bad and mediocre tee shots, perhaps, but since the definition of "good" becomes more demanding the better you get, surprisingly, the percentages stay the same. When leading tour pros hit 70 to 80 percent of fairways in regulation, everyone has to expect a fair number of "bad" tee shots.

In poker—say, for instance, five card draw—you wouldn't even look at your first card until you had all five. Who ever picked up all five cards and tried to figure out which one was dealt first? But the response above is as if you snagged the first dealt card in five card draw, saw it was a low card, and gave up on the game. Wouldn't that be a bit premature? It doesn't actually cost anything, even at poker, to see at least all five cards, and a whole lot of winning hands would be lost if you gave up after the first.

The least you can do is look at the first five tee shots, then decide whether to "throw in the hand." (Clearly this is also premature, but it usually works out that if we can get somebody to look at five holes before they judge the whole round, then enough has happened that is positive to make a good round possible.)

It would be more reasonable to assume that you are going to hit the same number of good, average, and bad tee shots as you have produced on average over your last ten rounds. In that case, a bad drive on the first could almost be viewed with relief, in the sense of "I got that one out of the way!"

You want to look at it as a childhood probability problem. There is a drawer with eighteen different pairs of socks. If you usually hit nine tee shots in a round to the fairway, then nine of the pairs of socks are green. If you hit four tee shots into the sand, then four pairs of socks are yellow. If you hit three into the rough, then three pairs of socks are light brown. And if you usually hit the other two tee shots into the trees, then the other two pairs of socks are dark brown.

Now, if your first shot on the first hole goes into the sand, you have removed one pair of yellow socks from the pile. That is one pair of yellow socks you no longer have to worry about, and your fairway tee chances on subsequent holes are slightly increased!

Of course, on this theory pushed to the limit, after nine "bad" drives you would be supremely confident—rather than your usual feeling of devastation—because as a past probability student you would know there are only nine remaining pairs of socks in the drawer. And you would know that, even though you cannot see them yet, they are all green!

If your negative thinking persists, you might think you're not going to hit nine fairways in regulation after four in the sand, three in the rough, and two in the trees. But even a negative thinker will admit that he is more likely to hit fairways if he thinks he has now exhausted his supply of bad shots. Those who think this way, by becoming more hopeful, or at least less disheartened, increase their chances of success.

Those who have been rocked and disheartened by each and every bad drive, who felt that the first predicted disaster, were more and more likely to hit badly, and were almost a lock to finish even worse than they started.

If we were flipping coins, it would be unusual to flip tails nine times in a row. But if we did, who would seriously bet that we would flip another nine tails in a row?

And this is very conservative. We are talking about nine bad driving holes in a row, which is unusual. Many players, after one or two bad driving holes, become desperate or desperately self-critical, which leads to the same results. In this case it is like flipping tails one or two times in a row, and assuming that means all eighteen coin flips will come up tails. Why would you make that bet?

2. "IF I START SLICING (OR HOOKING), THEN I'M FINISHED."

The idea behind this deadly thought is that our game is like a ball delicately poised at the top of a steep hill. If it veers off at all in any direction, then it will go downhill in a hurry.

Certainly, this is not necessarily true. It is very possible to hook or slice occasionally for subtle technical reasons that do not necessarily repeat themselves, but that, ironically, are more likely to repeat themselves if we believe this illogical thought. Because if we believe we are finished, cooked, ruined, about to be eaten by the saber-toothed tiger, then we will produce some chemicals out of fear and anger that will make it that much more likely that something like a slice or a hook will reappear on our next shot.

Another reason that it is not true that one slice or hook is followed necessarily by another is that there are certain situations (see Chapters 10 and 11) that elicit fight-or-flight chemicals that do indeed cause a slice or hook, but these situations are relatively few and far between, and between these situations a player may reasonably expect that the slice or the hook is not going to reappear.

Furthermore, it is possible to repair our defenses, or muster our physical defenses against psychologically induced hook or slice chemicals, and keep these enemies generally at bay.

So it is far from necessarily true that if you start hooking or slicing you are finished. You might as well think that if you burp you will never stop burping. It's possible, one supposes. If you burp, you may not like it and you may be momentarily embarrassed. But once you have burped, it is also quite likely that it is "out of your system."

3. "IF I THREE PUTT, MY ROUND WILL BE RUINED."

Basically, when you 3 putt you take an extra stroke that you had not anticipated. Of course, this happens all the time. We miss the green, or even hit the green but roll into the fringe. Then we chip and 2 putt. This is not exactly what we had hoped for, but it does add up to an extra stroke.

There is a trite saying that golfers often quote: "There are no pictures on the score card." They say this when someone, usually someone other than themselves, has hit a lucky shot. Usually, this is a shot that saves them a stroke they expected to lose.

When golfers lose a stroke they had expected to save, they would do well to remember that there are no pictures on the score card. Extra shots will be taken and saved all around the course. It is not logical to assign to a particular shot a make-or-break significance. Making the putt won't necessarily save the round, and missing the putt won't necessarily break the round. The total quality of the round is going to be determined in seventy or eighty or ninety different locations (those being the locations from which you hit the seventy or eighty or ninety shots that add up to the score for the round). No single one of them, on the score card, has a significance any greater than any other.

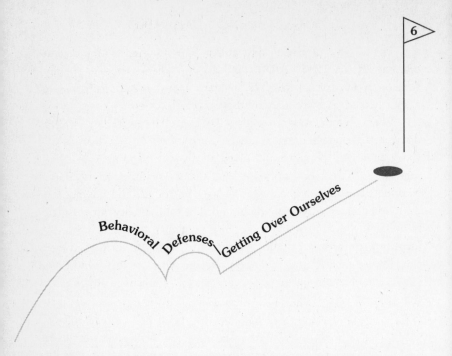

6

Behavioral Defenses\Getting Over Ourselves

BEHAVIORAL DEFENSES are completely different from insight defenses and cognitive defenses. Behavioral defenses do not involve any explanation, either internal or external, of our anxiety. With behavioral defenses, as the name implies, we simply change our behavior and everything else follows.

If we have a dog phobia, then behavioral therapy will suggest a number of strategies that enable us to prolong our exposure to dogs. When done properly, this will down-regulate our receptors and decrease our production of the chemicals that cause panic and anxiety. There's a certain amount of common sense to this approach (get back up on the horse and ride) and most people have noticed that as they progress in golf, their anxiety becomes somewhat less over time. This is because as we are exposed repeatedly to something that for whatever reason is frightening to us, we become progressively less and less afraid.

This is behavior therapy working without strategies; with strategies, the turning down of the anxiety response can be accelerated.

Behavior therapy teaches someone who suffers a panic attack every time they see a dog to tolerate one with no anxiety. You might say, "So what, dogs don't bother me." With behavior therapy, someone who gets a panic attack whenever they get in an airplane, or on top of a building, or inside a subway, can learn to tolerate these things without anxiety.

Perhaps none of this bothers you. But everybody has something that loosens the faucet on the panic/anxiety chemicals, letting them flow into the bloodstream. Do you doubt this?

Ask your friends to hold a snake or a cockroach in their hands. A cockroach is harmless, but how many of your friends will hold one in their hand? You see, everyone has panic/anxiety chemicals just waiting to be released. The problem is that it isn't necessary in the ordinary course of life to hold a cockroach in your hand.

But for those who play golf (and you do) it *is* necessary to tee off, to hit over water, to play against difficult people, and to putt. The problem is that if you are releasing some of these anxiety/panic chemicals in these situations, then it will be extremely difficult to execute these challenging shots. The chemicals cause you to do badly, and then you release more chemicals in the future. Bad results lead to justifiably increased fear about future results. And more fear means more chemicals.

Hazards on the course become saber-toothed tigers. These hazards, like the saber-toothed tigers of old, gain the ability to reflexively release our anxiety/panic chemicals.

Behavior therapy offers a way to turn this reflex off.

Unlike cognitive and insight therapies, behavior therapy is not about you thinking you see a saber-toothed tiger when you don't. Behavioral defenses are more about how you can adjust to a saber-toothed tiger without the anxiety response if you go about it properly. "Ho, hum, another saber-toothed tiger" means less chemicals and thus more range game.

The good news, if you want to look at it that way, is that everyone has panic attacks. You, like everyone else, contain within your body a faucet that, right now as you read this page, is shut. But if anything happens to open that faucet even a little bit, these anxiety chemicals will start to leak into your bloodstream. Your bloodstream is in fact a fast-moving stream, and it will float these chemicals throughout your body in less than a second. Your muscles have a receptor that senses these chemicals. When these chemicals stick their "key" in the lock of your muscles, then your muscles get tight and strong. (Unfortunately, that is strong for lifting heavy objects and swinging the heaviest primitive caveman clubs; strong is not the same as quick, as in clubhead speed.) When these chemicals stick their "key" in the lock of your lungs, you breathe faster. In the lock of your heart, they make it beat harder. In the lock of your mind, they release anxiety, anger, and fear.

Actually, they have quite a big ring of keys, and they can unlock other problematical areas of your body as well. They have a key to your eyes, which can change your focus from broad to narrow, from distant to close. They have a key to your ears, and can turn up the volume on distant conversations—just what you need in your back swing. The chemicals even have the key to your balance center, and they can turn the gain on your balance up or down.

This is all about your balance settings, which are different in different situations. If you are walking across a four-inch beam between the walls of the Grand Canyon, very subtle changes in contour will be telegraphed immediately to your brain and will register on your balance settings, which, with the bottom over a mile below you, are quite fine-tuned. If you step on a ball-marker, your brain will register it like an earthquake.

Meanwhile, if you are a professional football player breaking through the defensive line for a big gain, you will hardly notice if you step on an arm or a leg; if you are hit hard by a linebacker, you may right yourself and motor on with your attention focused downfield where further obstacles await. Your balance settings are at the other end of the spectrum where small doesn't matter, where what doesn't knock you down doesn't really register.

• • •

The fundamental lesson of behavior therapy is surprising. Everyone knows that if you keep getting up on the horse, it is a little less scary. But it wasn't until relatively recently that the rule of the "magic hour" was discovered. If you spend an hour in the presence of something that opens your anxiety/panic faucet, then you will tighten it.

This is fascinating stuff. If you hold the cockroach in your hand for an hour, the anxiety/panic chemicals will be exhausted. We will have started out panic-stricken, perhaps almost trembling, saying "I can't stand it." At the end of an hour we will be saying "Ho hum, are we done now, because I have better things to do."

Now, of course, you are not interested in cockroaches, at least as long as they are not crawling on you. But you are interested in the momentary burst of anxiety/panic chemicals that circulates with its ring of keys making changes in your body when you tee up, or hit out of the sand, or over water, or play a difficult match.

The answer of behavior therapy is deceptively simple. You have only to endure the anxiety-provoking situation for a "magic hour," and the chemicals will be turned down. Voilà!

The problem, of course, is that these particular anxiety-provoking situations do not last an hour. They often do not last a minute. They do their damage and then we are off to the next shot.

Often we find ways to deal with the anxiety-provoking situation. We want people to stand in a particular place, or we don't turn back as far as normal, or we stiff-arm the club. And out of this we find a way to turn down the chemicals for a moment.

But it turns out that in the long run we are really turning up the chemicals. How ironic! Because the corollary to the rule of the "magic hour" tightening the faucet is the Supreme Rule of Avoidance. Every time you do anything to avoid or to cater to these chemicals you loosen the faucet!

Here is how it works. Remember that you have a faucet in your body that releases anxiety chemicals. It is true that every time you spend an hour in the presence of something that would usually cause the release of these chemicals, then you will somewhat tighten down the faucet. But every time you avoid a situation that would cause the release of these chemicals you open up the faucet a little bit.

In ordinary life, it would work like this. Suppose you had a common phobia, for instance a fear of flying. Whenever you get on an airplane some of these anxiety/fear chemicals drip or flow out through your internal faucet, causing you to feel fearful and anxious. If the faucet is open a bit further, more chemicals will flow, so that your heart pounds and you feel like you have to get off the plane.

Now, every time you spend an hour with these chemicals flowing, you will close the faucet. This is easier to do on an airplane than with many other phobias, which is the reason why, although so many people have some flying anxiety, so relatively few actually have the full-blown chemical release that prevents them from getting on planes at all. Since people can't get off once the plane is in flight, they are compelled to treat their phobia by exposure to the chemicals. And since airplanes are necessary for most people from a practical point of view (with only a week's vacation, most New Yorkers can't take the Madden cruiser to California, and no one can take it to Hawaii), most people have a strong incentive to reexpose themselves to the source of the chemicals, and thus to keep turning down the faucet to some extent.

Why do we say "to some extent"? If someone with an airplane phobia (a loose faucet activated by airplanes) continually exposes themselves to airplanes, then according to our theory shouldn't the faucet be retightened by the repeated exposures? Yes, the faucet is retightened. However, with every attempt to cater to or lessen the chemicals the faucet is slightly opened. If the anxious flier picks a particular seat—the aisle, or the window—or business class, or the front or back of the plane, then the anxiety will be temporarily lowered, but the faucet will be slightly opened, and more anxiety will follow.

We picked airplane anxiety as an example because in some ways it more closely parallels a number of golf anxieties than other simpler phobias. A simple phobia of snakes or spiders is generally handled by merely avoiding the stimulus. This leads to a great outpouring of chemicals in the offending situation, but the offending situation rarely comes up and when it does, running away is generally satisfactory.

Players who become anxious in certain situations on the golf course are having a trickle of chemicals through their internal faucet. These chemicals, usually few in number, cause small changes in muscle tension, breathing, vision, and balance. But these small changes are more than enough to effectively decrease the chances of hitting a good shot.

Because the golfer continues to play, does not avoid the game completely, he is continually keeping the faucet from unscrewing altogether. But because he is exposed to the offending stimulus for only a few moments at a time in the ordinary course of golf, he is deprived of the opportunity to "close the faucet" by exposing himself to the anxiety-provoking situation for a "magic hour." Furthermore, anything he does to cater to the anxiety will lessen it in the short run but increase it in the long run. The efforts of the golfer are analogous to the efforts of the flier to pick a particular seat, occupy his mind in a particular way, drink or take antianxiety medicine, even avoid certain flights if possible.

The golfer who is anxious on the first tee will abbreviate his back swing because it feels safer. In doing this he may be momentarily less anxious than usual and able to get away with a satisfactory hit. Subsequently, however, he will be more anxious. That is why none of these little accommodations are ever ultimately successful. Further and further accommodation is required over time. Less back swing is more comfortable, but more chemicals from a more open faucet subsequently cancel that out. Now he switches to the 3 wood, or becomes concerned with where everyone stands. This temporarily helps, but again the faucet is further opened, more anxiety chemicals offset the temporary advantage afforded by the accommodation, and some further compromise is required. Most players continue alternately compromising and enduring, opening and closing the faucet. They never get well, but they never get really sick. And of course there are some whose faucets slowly leak more and more. They end up teeing off with a 5 iron, and even that ultimately starts to break down.

SOLVING THE PROBLEM

Those who have read this far know that the behavioral solution to anxiety is staying in the situation that causes the chemicals to flow for an hour.

Those who have played golf know that most of these anxiety triggers, or faucet openers, only last for a few seconds or a minute at most.

Some golfers get anxious as they stand over the ball on the first tee. But the slowest golfer in America isn't going to stand over his ball for an hour. The same is true for those who get anxious over some type of putt. Similarly, the shot over water or out of the sand may provide enough chemicals to ruin the shot, but the whole experience will only last on average thirty to sixty seconds.

In the office and on the golf course, we have been able to utilize combinations of biofeedback, video, and audio to simulate prolonged exposure in order to achieve the "magic hour." Variants of this are available to you.

THE HEADSET DRILL

Get one of those cassette recorders with headphones. There are many brands available now, some for as little as twenty dollars. For this first drill you can record applause, or even yourself clapping. You can liven it up with an occasional "You the man!" or "Way to go!"

Next time you go to the range or the putting green wear the headset and play your recording while going about your business. You can also do this while playing a hole or two, perhaps by yourself.

At first this provides a mild distraction. The idea is to do this exercise until you no longer pay any attention to the recording. You can also do this introductory exercise with music if you prefer. Although those who are blessed by being extremely musical, usually having perfect pitch, may not be able to do the music drill; they use a different part of their brains to process the music and have more trouble tuning it out. (If you have never been able to play music to go to sleep, then you should stay away from music in the introductory exercise.)

ADVANCED HEADSET DRILL

This is a great and daring drill, but you may want to master the simpler exercise above before trying this. Reading the chapter on Cognitive Defenses will be helpful also, since this exercise combines principles from both. Essentially, in this exercise you identify flash-thoughts, which pass through your mind in pressure situations, and then extinguish them using behavioral principles.

What to Do: Record the thoughts that go through your mind in pressure situations. Actually record them on the cassette tape.

We did this with Bill. Bill is an accomplished golfer with a single-digit handicap. In certain situations, in the presence of other golfers who are long hitters, he becomes "anxious for no reason." Bill is a good example, because this can happen to him in a number of situations on the course: first tee, sand, water, putting.

We have previously asked him to write down what thoughts come into his mind as he is about to hit on the first tee. They are fairly typical:

> Just get it into play.
> Don't mess this up
> Don't slice.
> Hit through it.

Now we ask him what thoughts he imagines the other people in his foursome have about him. He asks whether we mean before he hits, or after. We are interested in both.

At first he says there are no specific thoughts, which is typical.

We ask him to make up thoughts they might have, as if he is writing a screenplay about this event and the thoughts need to be formulated as dialogue. Once he gets started he has no trouble coming up with things the others might think:

> He's going to mess it up.
> Bill has trouble with this shot.
> There goes Bill again.
> Bill, what a dork!
> Why are we playing with Bill?

Now we ask Bill to read these thoughts onto the cassette. He records them, over and over (we want thirty minutes of tape, which can be played twice for a "magic hour"). As the process gets boring we ask him, like good directors in a play, to put more emotion into it, then to really ham it up. "Bill?? *What* a doooork!!!"

Now we ask Bill to play this tape at nongolf times when he has an hour to spend on it. He could be at home watching *SportsCenter*, on the train, in the car, at the gym. It doesn't matter. The point is that at first he is embarrassed by these thoughts, which means that they still have power over him. In the next stage, they are still able to distract him. Finally, and it doesn't take that many repetitions of the tape—maybe three to five—he begins to ignore them, to tune them out.

Then he is ready to play the tape while hitting at the range, while putting on the putting green, or while putting on the living room carpet. When the voices are tuned out, he is ready to play a round with his portable cassette recorder on. Soon he is paying no attention to the voices. And the next time he plays in the usual foursome, he has earned an unusual experience. The voices have lost their force, and he is free to play his range game.

This is a daring exercise because it goes so much in the face of common wisdom. It is often said that you should think only positive thoughts, yet this exercise records and plays negative thoughts ad nauseam. What sense does that make?

It would be nice if we could decide to think only positive

thoughts, and then do it. But while we can decide to think only positive thoughts, we cannot do it. Bill has decided to think positive thoughts a thousand times, but those above are the thoughts he has. They are his thoughts, and they are the ones that trouble him. In this exercise he is using a technique that he already knows to extinguish their force!

No, he doesn't know the vocabulary of behavior therapy—he doesn't know *graded exposure, flooding, extinction*. But this form of behavior therapy is as old as childhood, and everyone has learned its lesson.

Everyone who has children has noticed that there was a period of time, perhaps ages three to five, when they paid attention to what we said. Then everyone has noticed how in the six to eight range they learn to tune us out. We say do this or do that, but they just keep watching the TV or thinking about something else. They didn't hear us. When we were kids we did the same thing to our parents. You, like everyone else, have already learned how to tune out what you don't want to hear.

This is a great exercise because it is like riding a bicycle. Once you know how to do it, you don't forget.

You already know how to tune out what you don't want to hear, and now you can do it (again).

WHEN IT comes to golf, these are all words for the same thing.

These "imagery defenses" deal with accessing certain mental states while bypassing both insight and cognition. How relaxed would you feel lying on a sunny, deserted beach in the Caribbean? Whatever the answer is, your body must contain the chemical settings for this, just as it contains the settings for the saber-toothed tiger. Suppose you got bored on the deserted beach, took out your driver, teed up a range ball, and smoothly drove one out into the ocean. If you were in that situation your body would know without being told how to regulate everything it takes care of internally, including the chemicals for tension and anxiety. If your body could move the dials toward those more relaxed settings now, wouldn't you be better off?

Utilizing relaxation techniques, guided imagery, or hypnosis you can access and apply feeling states associated with past or imagined situations. From the point of view of deep within the body, where the chemicals are released, you are not in the same tee box with a saber-toothed tiger so there's no need to release the saber-toothed tiger chemicals. We can release the Caribbean beach chemicals instead. Hello, range game.

HOW TO DO IT—RELAXATION EXERCISE

Sit in a comfortable chair or lie on a bed. Focus on your breathing. Close your eyes and picture yourself inhaling relaxation, and exhaling tension, anxiety, fear, and anger.

Now tense the muscles of your feet as tight as you can. Tighten, tighten, and relax.

Now tense the muscles of your legs as tight as you can. Tighten, tighten, and relax completely.

Now the buttocks. Tighten, tighten as tight as you can, then relax.

Now make a fist with each hand. Squeeze, squeeze as tight as you can, then let the fingers relax.

Flex the shoulders and upper arms. Flex as tightly as you can, tighter, and then allow the shoulders to relax completely.

Now tighten the muscles of your chest, abdomen, and back. Tighten, tighten, and then exhale, allowing the body to sink into the chair or bed.

Tighten the muscles of the jaw and forehead, tight, tighter, then relax, allowing the jaw to gently open as the muscles go slack.

Tighten the muscles of the neck, tighter, then relax, allowing the head to rest on the chair or bed.

Now in your mind imagine a meter for muscle tension. If normal muscle tension requires a setting of 7 or 8 then this is perhaps a 3. As you relax, focus on an imaginary meter that displays the number 3, and tell yourself that as you take your usual grip on the golf club and prepare to address the ball you will be able to reset muscle tension to this level—3—whenever you wish. Imagine a dial-type meter in which you are able to move the dial from 7 to 3. As the dial moves, feel the tension flowing down your body like a liquid, down through your body and into the chair or bed.[1]

GOLF COURSE QUICK FIX

In a tense situation on the golf course, when you feel the tension taking over your body, this is an excellent "fifteenth club" to have in the bag. Everyone knows the feeling. Whether stepping into the tee box or about to hit over water or facing a three-foot putt, there is a feeling we all don't like to get. The most prominent aspect for most people is a tightness in the chest; for others it can be anything from stiffness in the arms to light-headedness or loss of focus. In any case, there is one quick fix available to all who have practiced the relaxation exercise.

On the golf course, close your eyes for an instant when no one is looking or when looking down to take your grip on the club. Imagine that you can feel liquid tension flowing from your head down through your trunk to your legs then out through the soles of your feet into the ground. The process should take less than two seconds.

You will get a pleasant surprise as you address the ball. You will feel as though the viscous tension that was clogging up your mind and your swing has flowed down into the ground. You will feel more relaxed, more loose—more yourself!

---

[1]These relaxation and self-hypnosis exercises are very powerful. They are best done for the first time with the assistance of an appropriately credentialed professional.

If you have never done this type of exercise before, or if you do these and experience any tiredness or confusion or other change, consult a fully qualified professional.

Drive it into the ocean. (*Photo credit Phil Lee*)

HOMEWORK (ACTUALLY RANGEWORK)

To practice this best you want to wait for a moment of relative tension on the range. Of course, "relative" is the key word, since even the tensest moment on the range is less tense than an average moment on the course. But look for an opportunity such as after a series of hooks, or slices, or shanks, or mishits. It doesn't matter what the moment is, but it is best if it comes at a time of relative frustration when the chemical factory is making a few (frustration) chemicals. At this point you practice this exercise, which will subsequently be useful on the course when you find yourself in the grip of tension, or when you find yourself fighting back against tension by steering.

Do the rapid relaxation exercise right there on the range, resetting your chemical meter to 3.

Then visualize driving the ball into the ocean. Picture yourself at your favorite beach. Bored with sunbathing, you decide this would be a good time to tee one up. Looking around you are surprised to find there is no one else on the beach other than a few distant bathers who are also teeing up. You spot a conveniently located ball sitting up on a tee and in a very relaxed way assume your usual position. The ball looks very white in the beach sun, and quite large. You take a full backswing, because you have all the time in the world, and languidly let it rip. Perhaps you momentarily wonder at being so relaxed, but then think to yourself with a smile that you can't very well miss the ocean, so why not be relaxed?

Advance techniques utilizing imagery defenses are presented in Chapter 23, The Pre-shot Routine.

SECTION 4: *Physical Defenses Against Anxiety Chemicals*

8

Physical Countermeasures

WHY DO we need physical countermeasures?

Mental defenses against anxiety on the tee are like immigration officials or police fighting crime. Even if the police are doing a great job, there will still be some crime. If immigration officials are doing a poor job, many people will slip across the border; if they are doing an excellent job then only a few will sneak in. Similarly, even the finest mental defenses will not keep out all of the anxiety all of the time.

Mental defenses are like immigration officials stationed between your head and your body. Their task is to turn back anxiety thoughts at the border, before they slip into your body to spread anxiety chemicals. Good mental defenses will only allow a manageable amount of anxiety chemicals to slip past into our bodies.

But good players will make physical adjustments in order to neutralize even this manageable anxiety. It is obvious that there is one good reason for doing this, but in fact there are two.

Since even a small amount can spoil a shot, neutralizing the physical effects of anxiety will improve shot-making. But the second and, in the long run, more important benefit is psychological. By decreasing the effects of anxiety on shot-making we subsequently decrease anxiety itself.

We can think of the percentage of shots that we hit that are acceptable as our batting average. The higher our batting average is, the less anxiety we will experience as we contemplate our next shot. If we can reduce the physical effects of anxiety on present shots, we will collect compound dividends in the form of decreased anxiety effects on future shots.

To reduce the physical effects of anxiety on present shots we need to look at what anxiety is, and at what physical changes are caused specifically by anxiety (as distinct from faulty technique in general).

"Anxiety" is the name that we give to the effect that certain chemicals have on the brain and the body. These chemicals float along in the bloodstream like little messages inside of bottles. When these bottles get to the brain, the brain reads the messages *feel anxious* and *feel threatened.*

The muscles of the body also open these bottles and read the portion of the message encoded specially for them. The message to the hands, arms, legs, and gut is the message that was delivered to the hands, arms, legs, and guts of our ancestors as they faced the saber-toothed tiger. The arms and hands tighten on the club as they read *prepare to club the tiger to death or run back to the cave.*

The desire to hit at something when we're threatened is over a million years old. As infants, our little tantrums astonish our parents, who would be battered and bruised if it weren't for the fact that, as infants, our little fists have negligible power. When we are two and three we still strike out and our parents find some way of training us out of the expression of our rage. Growing up we become more socialized, and as adults the better defended among us are hardly aware of the desire we inherited from the caveman to swing a club at whatever makes us anxious.

While this desire to hit something with the club whenever we are anxious can pollute any shot, it is particularly likely to affect the drive. The length and heft of the club and a situation that calls for the inflicting of maximum damage can bring out the caveman in anybody.

When we enter the tee box, we may be hopeful. But as we tee up the ball and contemplate with pleasure the fairway where we are (hopefully) going to hit it, and as we also contemplate with horror the dreadful looming hazards that threaten us (sand trap, water, trees), the old caveman chemicals are produced. The part of the hole that our primitive brain assigns the role of threat to becomes a saber-toothed tiger. We are tempted to run from it, or we want to kill it.

When we sense a "saber-toothed tiger" anywhere on the hole, there is this typical buildup of fight-or-flight chemicals in the body. Most people know the feeling. These chemicals have a predictable effect on the swing, depending upon our perception of where the threat is coming from. When we sense the threat as sufficiently distant, down the right or left side of the fairway, the urge to flee is strong. When we sense the threat as close enough to attack (the ball itself), we try to "kill the ball."

SYNOPSIS It's ironic, but a key defense against mental assault is not mental but rather physical. As we move from the range to the tee, our range game is under attack. Competition and fear send chemicals throughout our body, which cause physical changes. These changes, as we have seen, are the same physical changes undergone by the caveman upon sighting the saber-toothed tiger. Power is sent to the arms—to club the tiger to death—and to the lower body, to run away. These physical changes in the body are predictable. They can and should be overcome to some extent by physical countermeasures.

9

Physical Defenses on the Tee

YOU ARE on the tee and you still feel a little bit of those chemicals churning through your system. Some anxiety must have slipped by your defenses. But you can still counteract it: All you have to do is keep your wits about you.

When you step up to the tee and feel that extra anxiety and tightness in the arms or chest, the first thing you want to do is figure out what you are afraid of. The last thing you want to do is to tell yourself to calm down.

The common swing thoughts—"Don't be anxious" or "Be calm"—are a prescription for disaster. That thought acknowledges the presence of chemicals produced following the sighting of a saber-toothed tiger, but instructs the muscles of the body not to react to that menace.

What happens then is that some muscles remain "scared stiff" and some muscles force themselves to loosen as one would in response to a command such as "Drop your gun, and come out with your hands up!"

We end up not stiff as a board, but not flexible as a bullwhip either. What we end up with is a partially rusted chain; some links are too stiff and some links are too loose for effective driving.

If you become suddenly anxious in the tee box as you address the ball, then you are reacting as if you were a caveman who has just seen a saber-toothed tiger. And you are making scared chemicals. Pretending you are not scared will only do extra harm to your game. Instead, face it, you are suffering from:

GENERALIZED TEE ANXIETY

The golfer who is about to tee off is looking at the ball. As he prepares to hit, he is flooded by fight-or-flight chemicals.

These chemicals were designed to help the caveman club the saber-toothed tiger. The golfer, flooded by chemicals from a million years ago, is diverted from his normal swing into a swing that is more primitive, more muscled, and more suited to clubbing an animal than to hitting a ball.

Without realizing how accurate the description is, we commonly say, "He tried to kill it!" or "He tried to kill the ball!"

HOW TO PHYSICALLY COUNTERACT MENTAL ANXIETY CHEMICALS: WHEN THE TEE SITUATION ITSELF CAUSES ANXIETY

The caveman didn't fool around. He got the club directly on the saber-toothed tiger (at least the cavemen who lived long enough to have kids did, and those are the ones we're descended from). It may be comforting when "hitting at" the ball to know that we come by it naturally, but we still won't be very pleased with the shots. For peace of mind we must realize that whenever we feel the anxiety chemicals in the tee box, we must be prepared to begin our physical regimen that counters the effects of the urge to "hit at."

• • •

When we enter the tee box with a feeling of anxiety, we may already have it in the back of our minds to hit at the ball. That is why it so commonly happens that players who are about to hit at the ball have already teed the ball too far back in their stance.

If you want to hit the ball as soon as possible, you can't really have it too far back in your stance. The farther back it is the sooner you get your club on it. Of course, this is an analogy based on a saber-toothed tiger: If you wait around for it to make the first move, that could be disastrous. When you are treating the ball like a saber-toothed tiger you unconsciously want to smash down on it as soon as possible.

The desire to hit at the ball will also lead to poor setup; the club will be more in a "hammer angle" in the right hand, with the shaft leaned forward—all the better to club the life out of it. For certain other shots such as chipping (and certainly if the ball were alive and needed killing), this would be better position. But it is not a position that is conducive to good driving.

Poor setup. Shaft leaned forward. (*Photo credit Steve Dolce*)

Ideal setup. (*Photo credit Steve Dolce*)

The swing sign of "hitting at" is the steep angle of attack. To drive the ball consistently, the ball must be struck on a shallow angle of attack while the club head is traveling level and/or slightly upward.

KILL THE BALL NOT THE TIGER

In any anxiety-provoking tee situation, make sure that you shallow out your swing arc. Set up with your feet at least as wide as your shoulders measured from the inside of the heels. This wide base encourages a wide, low take away and allows you to coil your upper body fully behind the ball on the backswing. Additionally, this wide stance creates a longer flat spot on the downswing, increasing the chances of a square, level contact.

Calm drivers also position the ball well forward of center in their

Steep downswing arc—"killing" the tiger. (*Photo credit Steve Dolce*)

Low-level to upward arc. (*Photo credit Steve Dolce*)

stance, generally between the left armpit and the left toe. In a threatening situation the golfer must sometimes almost force himself to position the ball this far forward. The farther forward the ball is positioned, the better the chance of catching the ball after the bottom of the swing arc, perhaps even slightly on the upswing to minimize backspin for maximum distance. To encourage this, calm drivers generally tee the ball high and leave the tee in the ground after the ball is struck.

When there is any anxiety in the tee box, it is useful to visualize a low-and-level to upward impact with the ball and to swing freely through to the finish. Watch anxious players take practice swings with their driver and they invariably brush the grass or take a small divot. They are already "hitting at" something with their swing, rather than swinging through. When they repeat this motion, they are surprised to see the balls "skyed." They will then tee the ball lower to prevent the ball from skying. Teeing the ball lower is a sure recipe for steepness, and even more skying, and even more anxiety.

EXERCISES TO COUNTERACT HITTING AT THE SABER-TOOTHED TIGER

A calm professional's practice swing is an uninhibited, accelerating, "ground-free" swoosh and "air swing." To capture this "air swing" feeling, set up with your driver held just above the tee ball and intentionally whiff just above the level of the ball. Any steepness or "hit instinct" will result in contact with the ball.

Anyone who is still having trouble with a steep angle of attack in anxious situations on the tee should try this additional drill popularized by Jim McLean. In order to more firmly fix in the mind the physical antidote to "hitting at," hit half and ¾ shots with a teed 5 wood trying to sweep the ball and leave the tee in the ground.

Intentional Whiff Drill. (*Photo credit Steve Dolce*)

5 Wood Drill—note tee in ground. (*Photo credit Steve Dolce*)

Tiger on the Right: How Anxiety Chemicals Cause a Slice

THE MIND-SET WE WANT

Calm, enthusiastic drivers relish the idea of driving the ball. They enjoy launching the ball with a freewheeling, uninhibited swing. On a narrow hole with trouble on the right side, the calm, enthusiastic drivers see the trouble, but use it only as a criteria for selecting a target. Once the target is identified, calm drivers focus merely on where they want the ball to go, and never on how to steer the ball away from trouble.

THE MIND-SET WE'VE GOT

Wouldn't it be nice if it worked that way? But it doesn't. It doesn't work that way all the time for you, and it doesn't work that way all the time for us.

No matter how good your mental defenses are, there comes a

time when you are standing in the tee box looking down the right side of the fairway at a place you don't want your drive to go. It could be water, it could be sand, it could be trees. At that moment, though, it is what you are afraid of. At that moment you can almost see it eating your ball, eating your game. At that moment it is for you a saber-toothed tiger. One million years ago, your great-great-great-great-great-grandfather, with a club in his hand, looked down the right side of a clearing and saw a saber-toothed tiger. He immediately produced a bunch of chemicals, which helped save his life. Two of the main things these fight-or-flight chemicals did were to strengthen his arm muscles so that he could get a crushing grip on his club (fight), and galvanize his hips and legs so that he could if necessary get away from there in a hurry (flight).

When you allow your mind to think of that hazard on the right as a threat, you send a message to your body to make these same chemicals. You won't have the same sudden burst of fight-or-flight chemicals you would release if a real tiger, or terrorist, suddenly popped up on the hole. But even a sprinkling, even a pinch, of these chemicals in your bloodstream will have a predictable effect on your swing. You want to be ready for the physical changes these chemicals will make in your body so that you can counteract them. That may not be as good as not having the fight-or-flight chemicals in the first place, but it will be a whole lot better than leaving them to act unopposed on your body.

These chemicals will do the same thing to you that they did to your great-great-great-great-great-grandfather. They will tighten your grip on your club, and they will incite your body to run away. Either of these two changes can cause a slice. Together they have the ironic result of making us put our ball exactly in the one spot we sought to avoid—the hazard on the right.

Our muscles tense to strike the beast, while our hips and body try to run away from danger. In an effort to "steer" or "overcontrol" or "play safe," we usually miss the target right by a much wider margin than we would on a wide, comfortable driving hole.

How to Fix the Anxiety-Induced Slice

Tightening the grip on the club increases the likelihood of slicing right and meeting the tiger face-to-face.

The natural response of the caveman seeing a tiger is to tighten the grip on his club. On the golf course, this keeps our club from releasing (the toe passing the heel after impact caused by the proper rotation of the left forearm). The resulting open clubface both starts the ball out right of center and causes the ball to spin clockwise as seen from above (slice spin). The resulting shot, as we all unfortunately know, is a weak push-slice—starting out uncomfortably right and then, to our horror, continuing to drift further and further right until it ends in the very hazard we sought to avoid.

This is, in theory, the easiest problem to fix—take several deep breaths and simply monitor your grip pressure before and during the swing (about 4 on Jim McLean's scale of 1 to 10). If that works you're all set (and you can proceed to Run for Your Life, page 83). But if it doesn't, or works for a while and then stops working, you are having a negative thought problem and may enjoy the results of the Caveman Grip exercise.

Exercise for caveman grip

The problem comes because you are trying not to squeeze the club, and trying not to do things is never a good idea. It is important that we find things we seek to do or feel, rather than trying not to do something (e.g., not grip tight) or not to feel something (e.g., not feel anxious).

Think of grip pressure as being controlled by a sliding switch or rheostat in the brain. Focus on the switch itself. Take a golf club and swing it while focusing on turning up the tension in the hands and forearms. As you swing the club, experience the loss of swing feeling. Now focus on the rheostat as you gradually slide

Tight grip inhibits release of fore-arms. (*Photo credit Steve Dolce*)

Lighter grip pressure and WD-40 feeling allows forearms to rotate and release club. (*Photo credit Steve Dolce*)

the tension control switch down. Slide it down just enough to feel the swinging weight of the clubhead. Now keep gently swinging the club back and forth as your mind automatically memorizes the settings for being able to feel the swinging weight of the clubhead. The next time you are on the tee, don't bother with "practice swings."

Gently swing the club back and forth until you can feel it rotating on its own. Immediately before teeing off, vividly imagine a can of WD-40 (or any other rust-dissolving lubricant) being sprayed on your wrists and forearms. Feel the coolness and the slickness of the oil, and visualize the rust on your forearm hinges dissolving. Then tee off while maintaining the sense of experiencing the club rotation, and see this particular slice disappear.

Tiger on the right! Run for your life!

The other thing frightened drivers do when they see a tiger on the right is to twist the hips more quickly and violently to the left during the swing with the intention of not leaving the ball out to the right. This is the golfing equivalent of trying to run away, but this also has the paradoxical (Appointment in Samara) quality of making it more likely they will put the ball beside the tiger in the right-hand hazard. Another related cause of slicing under stress is attempting to avoid the tiger/hazard by turning the torso and arms rapidly to the left on the downswing. This golfing equivalent of trying to run from the tiger is often accompanied by aiming left of the target, "just to be safe." By aiming and/or swinging left of the target, the golfer is creating severe left to right spin (unless the club is severely closed). Even though the ball will tend to start left of the target, it will usually end up well to the right.

Additionally, by aiming left the player is subconsciously telling himself to slice to some degree in order to hit the target. Between the spin and the subconscious desire to slice slightly, the player almost always misses the target right—particularly if he is tight and lacks

Aiming well left of target.
(*Photo credit Dolce/Chen*)

Square alignment.
(*Photo credit Steve Dolce*)

Severe outside in "above plane" downswing, which creates left to right spin—caused by alignment and rapid rotation of trunk.
(*Photo credit Steve Dolce*)

On plane downswing.
(*Photo credit Steve Dolce*)

confidence. This self-fulfilling prophecy causes the player to aim further left on the next shot, further exaggerating the problem.

Fight-or-flight is the well-known name given to the chemical reaction we have when we encounter the saber-toothed tiger. The name accurately describes the gut reaction to either hit the saber-toothed tiger or run away from the danger. The picture on the left illustrates the clever though self-defeating way the golf swing allows us to do both at once. When the mind has picked out a particular object on the right to be the "saber-toothed tiger" (typically water, or out-of-bounds, or sand), the club can "hit at" while the hips "run away." Unfortunately, as you can see in the next picture, when the hips run away the club is dragged from right to left across the face of the ball. This causes the ball to spin clockwise. Ironically, this clockwise (slice) spin causes the ball, as we noted above, to squirt right at the very hazard we were seeking to avoid.

Over-rotated "slice" finish. Hips have "run away" from danger on right, and ball is slicing back into danger area. (*Photo credit Dolce/Chen*)

Professional finish. (*Photo credit Dolce/Chen*)

There is another "tiger" problem that can be caused by any of the three tiger problems (tiger as ball, tiger on right, and tiger on left) that we are discussing, but that also is common with danger on the right, particularly when there is an associated need to "kill the ball." (They travel together because one response to a tiger on the right is to kill the ball so that if we do go right we will go over the hazard.)

When players are trying to steer the ball, they fail to wind their bodies completely on their backswing. This causes them to rotate or move laterally their upper body excessively on their downswing to obtain clubhead speed. This puts the body in front of the arms too much and causes the club to be dragged across the ball with the clubface open. This also of course causes the ball to start straight and curve to the right.

**Advanced remedy: The complete physical cure
(suggestion: complete mental defenses first)**

Incomplete coil (face the tiger all the way, and don't turn your back). Makes for a long golf day, but, hey, the ball will never be able to pounce by surprise and eat you up. (*Photo credit Steve Dolce*)

Full coil. (*Photo credit Steve Dolce*)

All fears of the tiger on the right are at once both irrational and well-founded. They are irrational because there is in reality no saber-toothed tiger in the right hazard. They are well-founded because there is no absolutely safe way to play the shot so that you can be guaranteed avoiding the right hazard.

But if we go back to the concept of batting average, we begin to see a way to shoot our way out (to borrow a phrase from Bill Parcells). If we can find a physical way to dramatically decrease our risk of being in the right hazard, then we will be psychologically less anxious about danger on the right, and we can make this cascade or vicious cycle work for us rather than against us.

It's true that the more often we get into trouble on the right, the more anxious we are about trouble on the right. And as we have seen, the more anxious we are about trouble on the right, the more likely our ball is to veer to the right.

But the converse is also true. The less often we hit into trouble on the right, the less anxious we are about it; and the less anxious we are, the less often we hit into trouble on the right. One move that starts a decrease in frequency of misses right can ultimately result in our forgetting altogether about the saber-toothed tiger on the right.

One answer is obvious, and not as difficult as it sounds. We only have to let the ball curve left rather than right. We say *let* the ball curve left rather than *get* the ball to curve left, because you don't have to really do anything to make this happen. The intermittent slice that pops up particularly when you don't want it to ("I can't believe it! Just what I didn't want to happen.") does not result from a swing change, and therefore fixing it does not require a swing change.

And remember, even if the ball does not curve left, making one or more of these draw moves will physically counter some of the effect of fight-or-flight slice chemicals. By countering the effect of some of these chemicals, we get into trouble on the right less often. The less we get into trouble on the right, the less fear chemicals we produce when we see a hazard on the right. So these moves put us on the road to becoming the calm enthusiastic driver we were on the range, rather than the fearful overcontrolling driver we were when facing the hazard on the right.

PHYSICAL ANTIDOTES TO FEAR-INDUCED SLICE

To get the ball to curve left the player must effect a change in the clubface by any one, or better yet a combination, of the following:

1. Strengthening the grip (turning the hands to the right);
2. Lightening the grip pressure: see Caveman Grip (page 82), and note relationship between Caveman Grip and "blocked" shot; or
3. Learning to allow the forearms to release (see Caveman Grip).
4. Squaring alignment of the hips and shoulders, or perhaps even aiming slightly to the right of the target (creating the opposite spin).

Square alignment, perhaps even slightly right.
(*Photo credit Lee/Chen*)

Creates slight inside-to-out swing path.
(*Photo credit Lee/Chen*)

Allows player to start the ball to the right of the target
(creating hook spin). (*Photo credit Lee/Chen*)

Weak grip: one knuckle showing on left hand—V of right hand points to left shoulder. (*Photo credit Steve Dolce*)

Strong grip: 2 to 3 knuckles showing on left hand—V of right hand points as far right as the right shoulder. (*Photo credit Steve Dolce*)

Following these four steps will cure the slice caused by anxiety about slicing (i.e., the tiger on the right). If you have initiated the four steps but want to speed full results, then do the Turn back and swing through exercise below.

Turn back and swing through to cure slice

Particularly when threatened by a relatively close tiger/hazard on the right, players who tend to slice when anxious will try for a little extra power to "ensure" that even if they do slice, the ball will go beyond the hazard (usually a pond or trap).

In a misguided effort to gain more power many golfers move their upper body forward and/or unwind the torso too quickly on the downswing. This results in either the handle being pulled through impact ahead of the clubhead (a slice) or a compensatory premature flip of the hands resulting in a loss of power. The symptoms of this effort to gain power are very like the symptoms we have seen from the fear of danger on the right, and one exercise remedies both.

1. Pull your right foot back and slightly right.
2. Coil fully behind the ball.
3. Starting the downswing, delay the unwinding of your torso by shifting your left hip and knee laterally (toward the target), while keeping your head back and your right shoulder behind you, or fully wound, as long as possible.
4. Once you have the feel of steps 1 and 2, complete your downswing by feeling as if you swing your arms and clubhead past your head with minimal or no trunk rotation. Let the weight of the swinging clubhead swing past your torso to the finish and try not to allow your body to turn to the finish. This should cause the ball to hook.

On normal swings, think, "Turn back, then swing through," and feel as if the clubhead pulls your torso to the finish in incremental amounts until you achieve the desired ball flight.

Timing problems add to the two physical effects of fear we are discussing. When a golfer is nervous, anxious, or otherwise unconfident, it is difficult for him to time his swing properly. With a higher handicap player whose hands are less trained to release properly, the lack of loft on a driver will make the player under stress more susceptible to slicing, while the better player will tend to fight a hook (see next chapter).

Closed stance. Aim right, right foot back. (*Photo credit Steve Dolce*)

Full shoulder turn.
(*Photo credit Steve Dolce*)

Let the clubhead pull your body and arms to promote release.
(*Photo credit Steve Dolce*)

Let the clubhead and arms swing past your head and feel as if your body and shoulders have not turned, or your back has stayed to the target until after impact.
(*Photo credit Steve Dolce*)

---

14 BALL DRILL

Fourteen is a magic number on the driving range. That is because there are fourteen driving holes on the golf course after excluding the par 3 holes.

Pick out an area on the driving range roughly equivalent in width to the average fairway.

Then drive fourteen balls, keeping careful track of fairways hit. This is an important statistic, which is kept in all tour events. Multiply the number of "fairways" hit by 7 to obtain the percentage of fairways hit in your "round." This is also an important number.

Obviously, it is going to be a fun challenge to keep track of the number of fairways you can hit in the fourteen allotted tries. And of course you will want to try to improve on your score.

This is an excellent exercise for improving accuracy as well as for imposing "tee tension" on the driving range.

MENTAL MASTERSTROKE Perhaps the greatest value of the 14 Ball Drill is mental. This drill helps establish reasonable expectancy. If you hit eight fairways on the range, there is certainly no reason to expect to hit more than eight fairways on the course. The true value here is in not being thrown off your game by missing a fairway. Players who do not have reasonable expectancy can be spooked by missing a fairway or two and ultimately miss far *more* fairways than they would on the range.

PRE-SHOT ROUTINE

Practice on the range using your pre-shot routine and monitoring your relaxation and grip pressure. Try to make every swing with a consistent amount of preparation and effort, which will result in a consistent rhythm.

MENTAL MASTERSTROKE Play the 14 Ball Drill using pre-shot routines. When you find a routine that actually lowers your score, you will employ it because it works. Too many pre-shot routines are people doing things they think they ought to do rather than doing things that actually help.

SYNOPSIS Anxiety on the tee is not simply generalized anxiety. The mind has identified a particular threat, and is responding to that as if to a saber-toothed tiger—with either fight or flight. There is one tiger we attack, the ball, and this chapter reveals the physical changes that take place when we try to "kill" the ball, and how to counter them.

The two tigers we try to flee from are the tiger on the right and the tiger on the left. This chapter shows how to counter the physical changes caused by a hazard/tiger on the right, as well as how to ultimately eliminate that anxiety by following four steps.

Of course, eliminating the effects of tension and fear and reacquiring our natural ability to draw the ball when faced by a tiger on the right can bring its own higher-order problems (see Chapter 11: Tiger on the Left: How Anxiety Chemicals Cause a Hook).

APPOINTMENT IN SAMARA

Golf is sometimes like John O'Hara's story. In the story, a man sends his servant into the village to the market. In the marketplace the servant runs into the devil, who tells the servant, "I am coming for you later today." The servant runs home in fear. The master gives the servant money, and tells him to go hide in the distant city of Samara until this is all straightened out. The master himself goes to town and confronts the devil, saying, "We need to talk." The devil says, "Fine, but later. Right now I'm in a hurry—I have an appointment in Samara."

The lesson here is that the more you try to avoid some problems the more likely they are to occur. We have seen how trying to avoid a hazard on the right can make it more likely that a player (especially a mid or high handicapper) will hit into that hazard. In this section, we see how trying to avoid a hazard on the left can make it more likely that the player (especially a low handicapper or professional) will hit into that hazard.

Hands release. (*Photo credit Steve Dolce*)   Body release. (*Photo credit Steve Dolce*)

Under pressure, the lower handicap player tends to fight a hook. This is because his hands have been trained to release. In the best players, this is timed in sync with the rotation of the trunk (body release). In a less accomplished player, this release tends to happen independently of the body. Both releases can be effective, but the hand release is more difficult to time (and therefore more likely to malfunction under pressure).

The hazard on the left that threatens the drive accentuates the tendency to hook. When water, sand, or trees become a saber-toothed tiger, the chemicals again "frighten" our hips and legs, which want to stay away from the menace. In this case, rather than turn toward the dreaded area, the hips are frozen, shying away from the hazard they seek to avoid. Most commonly, lower handicap players hook when their bodies fail to rotate properly due to fear of trouble on the left side. Often the player blocks his rotation by trying to swing out to the right to keep the ball from going left. This momentarily "freezes" the hips, which allows the arms to release faster than normal. Any time the body slows through impact, the arms and clubhead, because they have swinging momentum, will pass the body and close the clubface.

Hips frozen, club flips over closed. (*Photo credit Dolce/Chen*)

Trunk rotation keeps club from closing too fast. (*Photo credit Dolce/Chen*)

MENTAL MASTERNOTE It is extremely important to note that "hips frozen" does intuitively appear to avoid trouble on the left, while proper rotation seems to be headed for trouble on the left. Examine the mind trap in these pictures carefully.

High or hook finish due to poor hip rotation. (*Photo credit Steve Dolce*)

Hips well left of target results in proper finish. (*Photo credit Steve Dolce*)

MENTAL MASTERNOTE Note how the high finish deceptively looks like it will avoid the tiger. Study the picture, trying to get the feel of holding the hips and club back, so that you can recognize what a dangerous feeling that is and discard it from your game.

Good keys when threatened by a tiger on the left are "turn to face the trouble" and "rotate the center as the club trails."

Closed or hook setup. (*Photo credit Steve Dolce*)

Square setup. (*Photo credit Steve Dolce*)

Another ironic cause of hitting left is aiming to the right. This delays the hips, slowing the unwinding of the body, and causing the hands to release much as discussed earlier. In a better player, this alignment causes right to left spin, which is easy to overdo and hook severely. Rarely will you see a successful tournament player closed to the target.

To avoid trouble on the left side, the top player must have a feeling of aggressively rotating his trunk to face what he fears most, the left. Additionally, the player's center must rotate and release, which will ensure that the club will not flip over through impact.

PHYSICAL EXERCISE TO COUNTERACT
FEAR-INDUCED HOOK

SCRAPE AND DRAG DRILL TO
PREVENT HOOKING

A common problem among advanced players is an overly inside-out swing path resulting in pushes, or hooks, and fat or thin contact from the too shallow angle of attack.

To obtain a feel for the proper angle of attack and the proper inside-square-inside swing path do this drill popularized by teaching legend Gardner Dickinson:

1. Place the club three to four inches behind the ball.
2. From there, using the body and arms, lightly brush the ground to impact, and continue scraping the club with slightly more pressure to the ground a full eight to twelve inches beyond impact. The club should go low and to the left as the player feels the scraping with a rotation of his hips and right shoulder.

It is crucial to feel that the "depth of the scrape" occurs post-impact and that the hands are passive as the club is "dragged through" by the body to the finish. Then hit balls with this scraping, body release, quiet hands feeling. The contact will quickly be more solid and should fly with less right to left spin, resulting in a more consistent ball flight. Recreate this feeling to tame a tiger on the left.

As the hips clear, be sure to drag the club artificially low and left for about eighteen inches beyond the ball. (*Photo credit Steve Dolce*)

THREE-LANE DRILL

Once you have committed to a particular ball flight, visualize the fairway as a three-lane highway—a drill taught to teaching great Jim McLean by his mentor, Al Mengert. If you fade the ball, aim to start the ball in the left third of the fairway and fade to the center lane. If you draw the ball, aim in the right lane and draw the ball to the center. Never aim out of the fairway where a straight shot will hurt you.

ADVANCED VISUALIZATION TECHNIQUES

You may find it highly effective to imagine two lanes of automobiles parked in the fairway. You "play a trick" on the occupants of the

When you fade, you make people in the left recrea-
tional vehicles duck before your ball bounces noisily
but harmlessly off of the center lane (thus eluding the
tiger on the left). (*Photo credit Steve Dolce*)

left-hand vehicles (when you fade) by aiming at them. As they duck,
the ball bounces harmlessly (but with a satisfying noise) down the
middle lane. Conversely, when you draw the ball, it is the occupants
of the right-hand vehicles who duck before your ball draws into the
center lane (safely eluding the tiger on the right).

As discussed in the chapter on construction of swing thoughts,
this variation gains effectiveness by including harmless aggression, as
well as by concretizing an out-of-golf activity.

12

Sand

THERE IS probably no shot in golf that routinely terrorizes the average golfer as much as a bunker shot. Yet professionals and low handicappers refer to this as the easiest shot in golf. What accounts for this large disparity in ability and confidence? Some of it is simply a lack of skill, because a bunker requires a full swing and whatever flaws you have in your normal full swing come with you into the bunker. Additionally, much of the amateur's failure lies in not having a clear understanding of how the club should work in a bunker. Finally, this lack of skill and understanding breed fear and tension, which ruin any chance of good technique.

Typically the amateur will set up too much like a chip or pitch, with the ball too far back in the stance and the hands leading. He will then take too small a swing and attempt to hit one or two inches behind the ball. If all goes perfectly he may strike a successful shot that encourages him to repeat this. However, this technique leaves no margin for error. All too often the player will catch the ball first, sending it rocketing over the green. This is the worst thing that can possibly happen and always results in a vicious series of events.

1. The player will never again take a full swing in a bunker for fear of going too far.
2. The player will attempt to hit farther behind the ball, but because his hands are leading even more severely, he will dig the club and the ball will go nowhere—especially with this new short, tension-filled swing, which contains a balloon flaw.

Hands leading at address: recipe for mediocrity. (*Photo credit Steve Dolce*)

Rocket shot over green—ball first contact. (*Photo credit Steve Dolce*)

MENTAL MASTERNOTE   Any tentative approach is disaster in the bunker. This includes even proper technique: Proper technique executed tentatively will fail in a bunker. Of course the chances for failure are greatly multiplied if the technique contains a balloon flaw. By balloon flaw we mean a technical error that blows up like a balloon under pressure from anxiety chemicals.

To develop consistency and confidence in a bunker, it is essential to learn to take the same constant, gliding "cut of sand" for all green-side bunker shots. To achieve this cut, the technique must be tailored to an individual's swing and ability. Whatever the technique, it must be free of balloon flaws.

Certain fundamentals apply to everybody. First, it is important to understand the design of the sand wedge. A good sand wedge will have significant bounce (trailing edge lower than leading edge).

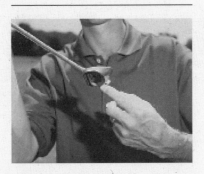

Bounce or back of club. (*Photo credit Steve Dolce*)

Proper bounce controls the amount of sand that is displaced and keeps the club from sticking in the sand. Most modern set wedges are difficult and have minimal built-in bounce. These wedges are versatile off tight lies but require incredible manipulation and skill for success by the average player in the sand.

To obtain the proper "cut" of sand:

1. Open your stance slightly.
2. Open and/or lay the club back slightly.

3. Play the ball far enough forward so that
   A. the trailing engine of the club hits the sand first (see Board Drill) and
   B. there is no danger of hitting the ball first on the way down.

Proper setup. This ball position is usually well left of center between the left toe and left armpit, but varies from player to player. (*Photo credit Steve Dolce*)

To get a feel for the bounce, hit a few balls off a painted 2×4 and try to get the paint on the trailing edge. (*Photo credit Steve Dolce*)

Now, place a ball in the middle of our anticipated cut of sand. If you've been taking eight-inch cuts of sand, you will enter three to four inches behind the ball and exit three to four inches past after going *underneath* the ball. If your first ball goes over the green, resist the temptation to be tentative and be sure you have the ball placed properly and that you go underneath and beyond the ball with your cut of sand. All too often people are tentative and stop their bodies, which destroys the club, arm, and body relationship (a balloon flaw). This causes the arc to shorten and the club to bounce up off the sand and into the back of the ball, sending it well over the green, and further increases fear and tentativeness.

Enter sand three to four inches behind ball. (*Photo credit Phil Lee*)

Underneath ball. (*Photo credit Phil Lee*)

Exit three to four inches past ball. (*Photo credit Phil Lee*)

Body stopping, causing club to bottom out, bounce off sand, and skull ball. (*Photo credit Phil Lee*)

Keeping the body going allows the club to go under and past the ball. (*Photo credit Phil Lee*)

MENTAL MASTERNOTE Practice a few minutes making your cut of sand without a ball and you will improve much faster. Then, even when the ball is there, try to focus on only two things: the cut of sand, and the bottom of the club that carves out that cut. Regard the ball itself as having no more significance than a spot of white light or a piece of cardboard on top of the projected cut of sand.

Mind-Body Exercise

Make three parallel cuts of sand without a ball. Then place a ball in the center of an anticipated fourth cut, and focus only on making a matching cut of sand, paying no attention to the ball itself. When comfortable with this, begin making two parallel cuts of sand without a ball followed by one with a ball. And when comfortable with this, begin making one cut without a ball followed by one cut with a ball.

MENTAL NOTE The ability to make a consistent cut of sand without a ball is the physical or technical requirement of the sand shot. The force that makes it harder to make the same cut with a ball there is the mental challenge of the sand shot.

MENTAL MASTERNOTE The biggest problem for amateurs in the sand is mental, but this does not refer to the anxiety and fear that accompany the shot! These are secondary effects that always accompany failure. The primary mental problem is a failure to properly visualize the shot itself. Study the Board Drill and rehearse in your mind a swing in which the trailing edge (not the blade) flattens out a ribbon of sand. Then visualize a club that is comprised entirely of a shaft attached only to a trailing edge, with no blade and no face. Practice in your mind swinging that through the sand, and use that image in the bunkers.

After mental practice, go to a bunker. Make several full practice swings and try to make divots four to eight inches long in the sand. Experiment with opening the blade in varying amounts to get a feel for the club gliding and not digging through the sand.

The more you open the clubface, the more "bounce" you create and the less the club will dig. Take care to make the divot long and relatively shallow with consistent depth before and after the ball. This "cut" of sand will vary depending on the texture of the sand and the skill and strength of the player. Accelerate to a full finish and try to make the sand fly out of the bunker. On the downswing, focus on turning your hips fully and using proper full-swing footwork as well.

Intended area of sand to be displaced. (*Photo credit Steve Dolce*)

Full relaxed finish. (*Photo credit Steve Dolce*)

DISTANCE CONTROL

Speed, tempo, and length of finish control distance. Trying to control distance any other way is another balloon flaw: Add anxiety and it will blow up.

After mastering this cut, make full swings of varying speeds and rhythms to see how far the ball travels on a given swing. Then take several full-length, medium speed swings with the same cut. This should produce a shot of ten to twenty yards, the "bread and butter" bunker shot. Practice this until you are very good at this technique.

Then calibrate a "maximum" blast distance with a full, hard swing.

**MENTAL
MASTERNOTE**
Visualize the cut of sand floating the ball out to the target—as if the ball is getting a magic carpet ride on the cut of sand. When you can visualize yourself cutting and launching a magic carpet of sand toward the green, your friends will see you as a sand genie.

After the maximum blast calibration, take full swings at progressively slower speeds. For the shortest of shots, you may feel you are stopping your finish somewhat shorter than usual. However, always strive to take the same cut of sand (or same size strip of carpet).

MIND-BODY NOTE
The image is of throwing the same size carpet of sand various distances by varying the speed and rhythm of the downswing and resulting length of finish.

Do not shorten your backswing (a balloon flaw), as this only increases the chance of your hands leading excessively, causing either the ball-first or the digging contact.

WHEN TO VARY CLUBFACE ANGLE

Conventional wisdom often states to open the blade for shorter shots and to square or even close the blade for the longest of shots from the bunker. However, when you open or close the blade, you increase or decrease the effective bounce angle of the club.

This may result in the club bounding off the sand (too open), causing the ball to go too far, or in the club digging (too closed), causing the ball to go too short. Either adjustment drastically changes the depth of your cut of sand, making consistency and feel difficult to achieve.

Except for the most specialized shots, the clubface angle is determined entirely by the texture and amount of sand in the bunker.

Short backswing = Bad idea. (*Photo credit Steve Dolce*)

Wide open face = Bad idea. (*Photo credit Steve Dolce*)

Hitting farther behind ball = Bad idea. (*Photo credit Steve Dolce*)

Control the distance with the length of your finish. (*Photo credit Steve Dolce*)

SHORT

MEDIUM

LONG

MENTAL NOTE Think of the flange or bounce of the club as the depth controller on a submarine. When you dial it to clockwise (open), you schedule a shallow dive; when you set it in the counterclockwise (closed) position, you are scheduling a deeper dive. Alternatively, think of yourself as taking two slices of carpet of equal length, but one is a thin piece of carpet, and the other is a thick or shag piece of carpet. (The closed setting tries to extract a thick shag carpet slice.)

Wet, firm, or thinly layered sand on a firm base requires a square to slightly open clubface to minimize bounce and still allow the club to dig slightly to get under the ball. Because of the reduced loft (by squaring the blade) and smaller amount of sand available to displace, the ball comes out lower and faster and requires a slower swing. Soft or deep sand requires a more open/laid-back clubface to increase bounce and keep the club from digging too deep. Because this adds loft, you will need to swing harder to throw the sand and ball a given distance.

MENTAL MASTERNOTE As with hooking and slicing, what is required here is the polar opposite of what many people intuitively feel. The sight of "concrete"—wet sand—makes people feel they must really muscle it, while the soft and powdery modern bunker seems to invite a correspondingly soft swing. Mentally rehearse the swings and bounce settings both in wet and in soft sand while referring back to the preceding paragraph until the intuitive feelings are erased.

THE TOUGHEST SHOT IN GOLF

For shots outside the maximum blast range, the player has several options. One method, useful for low clubhead speed players, is to strike the ball first or clean with a pitching style technique. This requires considerable skill and nerve. Another method is to skim a shallower cut of sand and/or strike closer to the ball. This also requires tremendous skill.

Often the simplest method is to blast the ball with a pitching wedge, 9 iron, or 8 iron using the normal green-side sand wedge technique. This is easier if a player's short irons have a similar design and bounce angle to the sand wedge. Shots beyond the reach of a blasted 8 iron should be played with the pitching technique mentioned above.

MENTAL NOTE The important mental point is that—unlike the green-side bunker—this is a difficult shot that you cannot realistically expect to make with frequent success. You don't get angry or frustrated if you miss a thirty-foot putt, whereas you may be perturbed if you miss a thirty-inch putt. If you fail to appreciate how difficult some shots such as the long sand shot are, then you will be setting yourself up for inappropriate anger and frustration chemicals. These chemicals will not be dissipated by the time you get to your next shot, and you know what happens then. The ballooned series of scores on the card almost always signals a series of unopposed and uncontrolled chemical releases, often triggered initially by unrealistic expectations about a difficult shot.

13

Chipping and Pitching

ANY PLAYER seeking to lower his score must develop a reliable wedge game. Knowing you can consistently get up and down in two shots takes mental pressure off your iron game and effectively doubles the target area on your approach shots.

Unfortunately, the majority of amateurs are more likely to hit the green from 125 yards than they are from 35 yards because of poor practice habits, bad technique, anxiety, and misconceptions. Many amateurs are taught routinely to lay up to full shot yardage or to carry multiple wedges with lofts as high as 65 degrees. Have you ever seen how far over a green a full swing lob wedge goes when skulled? If you own one, then of course you have.

Other players are told to lay up to one hundred yards, or full wedge distance. Under most conditions, from thirty-five yards out a competent chipper is going to beat anyone who is over sixty-five yards from the target. But by the way, what guarantees do you have that you'll lay up to perfect "full" swing yardage?

Instead of avoiding the dreaded ½ wedge, learn it!

This chapter is by far the most technically generic and detailed. Why? Proper wedge play is extremely simple and efficient if taught and learned properly. Most poor wedge players will tell you that it's "all in their head" or they have bad nerves or no confidence. Almost always it's not all in their head, although they are nervous and unconfident because their technique is so bad.

MIND-BODY NOTE This lack of technique and resulting lack of confidence are usually caused by misconceptions about how high the ball should fly near the green and how to make it go the desired trajectory.

This is particularly true when the player is going over a hazard such as a bunker (particularly if he's not a good bunker player). It can also be particularly true if the player is attempting to pitch the ball over an intervening obstacle with a club with too little loft, such as a modern 48 degree pitching wedge.

MIND-BODY NOTE Anxiety over the hazard, or using a club with too little loft, cause the player to try to add loft to the club and lift or scoop the ball into the air.

We're discussing basic pitches, the foundation of a successful wedge game. Almost always the player has more green to "work" with than he perceives and is trying to play a shot with too high of a trajectory (and risk—never forget that a higher shot requires a bigger swing).

MENTAL NOTE Many, many golfers try to hit the ball higher over bunkers than they would over rough. No defensive end is going to leap out of that bunker and stuff the shot. Sure, you wouldn't want to come up short and plop into the bunker, but with fifteen feet of grass between you and the green you wouldn't want to come up short and plop it into the grass either. Once there is a bunker or water underneath, we panic a little bit

No defensive end will block your shot.

and try to hit it a little higher. The subconscious feeling is that higher is safer. The truth is the opposite: The higher shot is the more risky shot.

Once again, fear chemicals cause us to do something that feels intuitively safer, but that makes it more likely that our ball will end up precisely in the place we were trying to avoid—in the trap or rocketed over the green. One analogy is to swimming. Swimming in water sixty feet deep may be perceived as scarier than swimming in water six feet deep. And if you are doing something extra with your stroke over the deeper water, trying harder to keep yourself up, then ironically you are not swimming as well.

This adding loft *whether intentional or subconscious* is what causes the number one fault of poor wedge players—allowing the clubhead to pass the hands during the stroke, which causes the swing arc to bottom out prior to impact, resulting in unsolid contact and

No reason to change trajectory of shot here. (*Photo credit Dolce/Chen*)

poor control of the loft and direction of the clubface. This leaves the player at the mercy of his lie, nerves, and luck.

MENTAL NOTE   Allowing the clubhead to pass the hands is a balloon flaw—a chipping stroke that contains this flaw can be managed on the range but will blow up under pressure.

To improve, the player must learn to use a club with its true loft—which requires a technical discussion.

When a top-notch player hits a full short iron, he arrives at impact with his weight primarily on his left foot and his hands leading the ball at impact, thus setting up a crisp descending blow. Such an impact takes quite a bit of skill, talent, and practice to achieve—unfortunately, many will never consistently achieve this in their full

 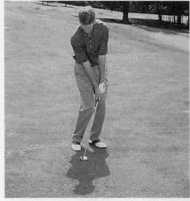

Full swing impact. (*Photo credit Steve Dolce*)   Chip impact. (*Photo credit Steve Dolce*)

swing. But there is good news! Solid pitching and chipping impacts are infinitely easier to achieve because we get to cheat by presetting and maintaining our impact position throughout the stroke.

The shots we will discuss here are chips and pitches ranging from about thirty feet to approximately forty yards. A chip shorter than thirty feet with a good lie is merely a putting stroke from a chipping setup with minimal body motion. A pitch beyond about forty yards gradually begins to assume the elements of a full swing from a pitching-type setup.

To achieve consistently solid, crisp contact:

1. Start Left
   A. With your stance narrow, place your weight 60 to 80 percent left at address. You should feel a slight pressure in your left hip and heel.
   B. Position the ball in the middle of your heels, taking care that your center, sternum, is left of the ball.
   C. Place the hands opposite the inside of the left thigh. This creates a targetward lean of the shaft, which presets a descending blow.

Setup. (*Photo credit Steve Dolce*)   Stay left. (*Photo credit Steve Dolce*)

D. Set up with the shoulders square and the stance open left of the target. You have now established your center, arm, wrist, and club-face relationship. Your next priority is to:

2. Stay Left

To ensure a crisp, solid descending blow, you must not allow your center to drift behind the ball on the backswing. To prevent this, allow the weight to stay in the left heel and hip socket. As you begin and complete the backswing, the right knee must stay in its original position with no lateral drift to the right. Feel a more descending arm swing and wrist cock partly due to the absence of weight shift. Minimize hip and shoulder turn due to the open stance and ascending arm swing.

HOW TO FIX IT

DRILL #1

Hit short pitches with the right heel in the air and the right toe down for balance.

DRILL #2

Hit pitches with a 2×4 laid perpendicular to your target line about twelve inches behind the ball and try not to strike it on your backswing or downswing.

Miss the 2×4. *(Photo credit Phil Lee)*

Turn left. (*Photo credit Steve Dolce*)

At this point, you have maintained the center, arm, wrist, and club relationships established at address. To preserve these relationships through to the finish:

3. Turn Left—Feeling
   A. Your center rotating around your left hip socket and heel as your hips turn left.
   B. Your upper left arm resting comfortably on your chest as you approach impact and finish.
   C. Your right heel rising and your right knee releasing diagonally toward the ball and target as your hips turn.
   D. A firm-wristed sensation of scraping the grass beyond the ball through impact and the club staying low early into the finish, rising only as the body turns with no wrist breakdown.

Scrape the grass. (*Photo credit Steve Dolce*)

During the downswing, the player must feel as if he is "resisting" the clubhead passing the hands by keeping the center and arms moving left and the hands quiet, resulting in a flat wrist at impact.

DRILL

To achieve this feel, set the club at address and merely turn left with the hands leading the club and firmly scrape the grass with the clubhead six to ten inches into the finish. There should be a definite feeling of the club being at its low point after impact with no cupping of the wrists.

Different length motions.
(*Photo credit Steve Dolce*)

DISTANCE CONTROL

Distance is controlled by club selection and length of backswing. The backswing must always be long enough to provide adequate power for an unhurried, non-handsy stroke on the downswing.

To achieve distance control, practice hitting shots with no specific target in mind. Merely focus on the length and rhythm of motion and take note of where the ball lands.

MIND-BODY NOTE This eliminates the subconscious downswing compensations the brain tells us to make for what it may perceive as the wrong backswing length. For example, a perceived too-short backswing causes a hurried or a flippy, wristy downswing to create additional power. Conversely, a perceived too-long backswing causes our center and arms to slow down through impact, causing the clubhead to catch up prematurely and pass the hands.

After rehearsing swings of various lengths you will begin to see the effect on distance. Then maintain sound technique and consistent rhythm.

Once you have become familiar with and practiced the elements listed above, you can simply recall the fundamentals by thinking "Start Left, Stay Left, Turn Left."

MENTAL NOTE On the course use your eyes to see, feel, and hit the shots. Take frequent looks at the target— create a vivid image in your mind's eye. Let your eyes tell your subconscious how big of a swing to take by staring at the spot you want the ball to land. Practice your technique enough so that your on-course motion is merely a reaction to the target, not a series of mechanical steps.

DISTANCE DRILLS

1. Practice trying to land balls on a small towel—hit the same spot with your sand wedge and 9 and 7 irons—note the distance the ball rolls.
2. Make practice swings while staring at the target.
3. Drop eighteen balls in various lies and distances. Putt out. Keep score.

Try to land on towel with different clubs for different results. (*Photo credit Steve Dolce*)

Stare at target. (*Photo credit Steve Dolce*)

14

Putting

THE LOSER'S ATTITUDE

"How did you play?"

"I played great—just didn't have any luck with the putter."

This is a common response to that question. It somehow suggests that putting is not a vital aspect of playing golf, but a game of chance tacked on the end of what is otherwise a skill game.

This is a loser's attitude.

If you putted badly, you played badly. Putting is an integral part of playing, unless you don't keep score, in which case you're not reading this book. This is an attitude that looks down on the player who has a mediocre day from tee to green, but salvages a good score by putting well.

Many people would rather complain about poor putting than actually practice and improve it. They fear being labeled a good putter or, worse yet, a scrambler. News flash!—Winners scramble. It's what allows them to stay close when they're not striking full shots well, and it's what allows them to bury you when they're on (Tiger Woods, 1997 Masters).

The good news about putting is that the stroke is fairly simple, requires minimal strength, and is a shot that players of all abilities can theoretically master. Only poor eyesight, unsteady hands, or a faulty conception can limit progress.

The most common cause of poor putting is neither "mental" nor "physical." It is a lack of experience caused by limited practice (compared to the amount of time spent hitting full shots).

MIND-BODY NOTE   A common mental cause of poor putting is tension caused by expectations about whether a putt should be made or not. Only mid-range putts are exempt. Below five feet, the shorter the putt the more tense a player becomes. The emphasis goes from rolling the ball over a spot to making sure they do not miss. On long putts, over twenty feet, the emphasis goes away from making a good stroke to trying to avoid a 3 putt.

The third cause of poor putting is **balloon flaws** in the putting stroke, idiosyncratic methods that may work on the putting green but that blow up under pressure.

How to fix it: Eliminate balloon flaws

THE TECHNIQUES THAT WORK

There are many successful ways to putt. However, there are certain traits common to great putters.

Set up with shaft and the ball forward and hanging at a 90 degree angle or slightly more (hands ahead). The worst putters tend to have the hands back, which inhibits a smooth take-away and puts a poor roll on the ball. Any motion that stays "inside the lines" (see shaft/alignment drill) and keeps the left wrist flat through impact has a good chance for success. Try to use the pen-

Proper setup. (*Photo credit Steve Dolce*)

dulum formed by the arms and shoulders. It is not a big problem if the wrists set slightly on longer putts, as long as the wrists stay set—flat left wrist—through impact.

It is imperative to use a rhythmic stroke that is neither decelerating nor rapidly accelerating. The putter can travel straight back or slightly inside on the backswing and straight through or back to the inside on the downswing. It doesn't really matter as long as the blade is square to the target and the club's path is momentarily down the target line (to minimize sidespin) at the moment of impact.

Shaft/alignment drill. (*Photo credit Steve Dolce*)

A SIMPLE DRILL TO CONTROL DIRECTION

Improves:

1. Alignment—use clubs to align blade, feet, eyes, and shoulders.
2. Optics—lets you see what straight looks like—important to set up and stare at target while using guidelines.
3. Let the 2×4 guide your clubface and path of club control.
4. Finish—hold and evaluate.

DISTANCE CONTROL

To obtain proper speed and a pure roll on putts, it is critical to control the ball's distance by the length of the stroke. Therefore a constant rhythm must be achieved on all putts. Poorer putters tend to take the same length backswing for all putts and strike the ball with various rhythms and amounts of force. On longer putts they must hit exceptionally hard and on shorter or downhill putts they have to slow down or decelerate to control the ball's distance.

Many players have been told to take a short backswing and accelerate through with a long finish to the target. This is an absolute rhythm and feel killer. To achieve a consistent feel-oriented stroke it is absolutely necessary to control distance with a constant rhythm and variable length of stroke. Therefore, the longer the putt, the longer the backswing and resulting finish. Although not technically true, it is often useful to feel that the follow-through length matches that of the backswing, but never finish artificially long. Sense a swing of the clubhead, not a sudden acceleration or deceleration.

MENTAL MASTERSTROKE Never refer to a putt left short/long as hit too soft/hard; refer to putts left short as needing a longer stroke and putts too far as needing a shorter stroke.

MENTAL NOTE The short backswing on the putt is often a disguised attempt to control anxiety. As such it is a balloon flaw: It may work when there is no anxiety to control, but it blows up under pressure.

MENTAL MASTERSTROKE Visualize rolling a ball to the hole with your dominant arm, feel the fluidity of that rhythmic, rolling motion.

DISTANCE DRILLS

Try humming to yourself when you putt: If you change your tempo you'll change your tune. Hit putts while looking at the hole on the course. Take your practice stroke while looking at the cup.

You already know how to roll a ball to the hole. (*Photo credit Steve Dolce*)

MENTAL NOTE Let your eyes tell your subconscious how long a stroke to take—remember, the rhythm is constant.

---

5 BALL X DRILL

1. Stroke a ball approximately three to four feet.
2. Double that distance by lengthening your stroke.
3. Triple that distance by lengthening your stroke, etc. Change only length and observe the ball's roll.

5 ball × drill. (*Photo credit Steve Dolce*)

MENTAL NOTE The key idea here is that you change the length of the stroke and observe how far the ball rolls, rather than changing the stroke to achieve a certain distance. If you make enough putts, preferably without any target, using various lengths of stroke, you will pick up a natural sense of how far balls roll. This is what you have already when you roll the ball with your hand.

READING GREENS

Assuming reasonable eyesight, the reason many players cannot read break properly is that they either lack sufficient experience or they fail to observe the roll of their ball and how much it actually breaks. Many people are unaware of simple facts like the ball breaking more on faster and/or downhill putts.

The deciding look is taken along intended line, not at cup. (*Photo credit Jeff Warne*)

The number one factor in reading break is determining the overall slope and drainage of the green. This can usually be determined as the player approaches the green from the fairway, getting a better overall perspective of the green and the general scope of the terrain where the green is located. The next step is to make a quick circle around the perimeter of the putt (preferably before your turn to putt), paying particular attention to the terrain between the ball and the cup.

The final and most important look is from directly behind the perceived line.

| **MENTAL NOTE** | Visualize the green being made of cement. Which way would a large volume of water drain |

off that green?

| **MENTAL MASTERSTROKE** | For proper speed on uphill and downhill putts, "trick" yourself into a longer or shorter stroke |

Which way would this water drain? (*Photo credit Phil Lee*)

Downhill. Imagined target, actual target. (*Photo credit Steve Dolce*)

Note that "center of cup" becomes the point on the high side where the ball actually enters the cup. (*Photo credit Lee/Warne*)

by visualizing the cup farther from you than it actually is on uphill putts and closer to you on downhill putts.

It is critical to carefully observe the area you believe you need to start the ball over as well as the effect of any sidehill slope you may be standing on while stroking your putt. For instance, a ball well above your feet will tend to start more left than you might expect, thus magnifying a right to left break.

NOTE   Almost all amateurs under-read break, particularly on fast greens.

Remember, on a breaking putt, the center of the cup changes. The "center" you are aiming for faces the direction the breaking ball will be coming from—it is not the apparent center that faces you as you line up.

Finally, particularly on Bermuda green, grain (the direction the grass grows) can have an effect on the curve and speed of a putt. This can be a tricky element as severe grain can make a ball seemingly defy gravity. On Bermuda greens, the grass tends to grow toward the setting sun. On northern greens, the grass can grow toward the nearest water and/or the sun. When putting with the grain, the grass will appear shiny; when against the grain, the grass will appear dull.

Having said this about grain, remember that the slope of the ground will have the most effect on the ball. The quality of greens today is such that the grain will rarely be a dominant factor.

MENTAL MASTERNOTE After quickly assessing all of the criteria (which takes a good deal of practice and experience), the most important element of a successful putt is total commitment to rolling the ball down the intended starting line or over a spot. Any indecision will lead to a subconscious adjustment resulting in a compromise. Commit to starting the ball over the intended line and trust your instincts. If you have any trouble with this, see the chapters on Visualization and Commitment.

MENTAL MASTERNOTE Great putting is about reducing our expectations about the result, thus lowering our anxiety. This allows us to perform at our highest level (the way we putt when no one is around). Brad Faxon said he became a great putter when he stopped caring whether they went in. Watch him—it's true.

EXPECTATIONS DRILL

Hit twenty putts of six feet from different angles—use your normal pre-shot routine—no repeats. What's your percentage? On the course, keep these expectations in mind.

An excellent drill to see the actual break. (*Photo credit Steve Dolce*)

MENTAL MASTERNOTE — Never tell yourself you *must* make it.

FURTHER DRILLS

Hit putts scattered around the hole.

Don't line up. On one leg or with one hand—amazed at how many you make?

Putt to tees—small target increases focus, makes cup look huge.

Hold finish for immediate improvement. (*Photo credit Steve Dolce*)

MENTAL MASTERY TONIC FOR ANXIOUS PUTTERS The single best piece of advice for anxious putters is to hold your finish and evaluate it. This almost always provides miraculous results. Why?

1. If you can hold your finish, then you had a finish—an improvement for most bad short putters.
2. This distracts you from worrying about results.
3. This provides feedback to evaluate.

OVERALL MENTAL ASSESSMENT This technique tricks you into a good stroke by emphasizing process over results.

Finally, it is important to have a consistent performance-enhancing attitude over every putt. The best putters walk in on their intended line and focus on where they want the ball to go—not where they don't want to miss it. And because they have no balloon flaws in their stroke, a little anxiety will not break down their putting motion. Remember, the great players are all great putters—and they know it.

It is the opposite of a vicious cycle. Knowing you are a great putter gives you confidence. And confidence helps you putt better.

Practice the thoughts and exercises in this chapter and you will become a great putter, and you will know it. You'll enjoy the confidence that gives you. Your opponents will repeatedly remind you that they just weren't as lucky on the greens as you were, but you will know the truth.

SECTION 5: *Putting It All Together*

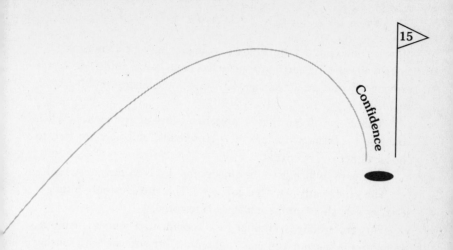

15

Confidence

THERE IS a general sense that confidence is a natural gift, like absolute pitch or charisma—some people have it, some people don't.

Which generally means some people have it, and I don't.

But people who believe this do not understand the fragility of confidence. John McEnroe, the greatest tennis player of his time and now an outstanding tennis commentator, has said that confidence is something that can be gained and lost several times in the course of a point.

A tennis player who has lost confidence in his topspin backhand should try to prolong a rally in which he hits three or four "safe" slice backhands. In tennis, if the flat serve isn't going in, the player would be well advised to safely spin a few into the box, building confidence, then go for the big flat serve down the middle.

What usually happens is just the opposite. Tennis players who are frustrated go for bigger and bigger shots, with more and more disastrous results.

Golfers will recognize this syndrome in which the caveman part of us becomes angrier and angrier, swinging harder and muscling the club, while the Upstairs part of us becomes more and more disapproving of our performance. This state, the angry funk, can be avoided.

A shot that doesn't work precedes a loss of confidence. When you lose confidence you are at a crossroads, and you are free to choose either of two paths.

One path, which is to "go for more," leads to the angry funk.

The other path is to "go for less." This involves only hitting a series of safe shots until confidence is restored.

This crossroads is familiar in all competitive games. In poker, after losing a big pot you can "tighten up" or you can start betting wildly, trying to get it all back.

In backgammon, after getting gammoned at the 8 level you can settle in to "grind it out" or you can "crack" and start "steaming," offering the cube too early and "actioning it up." If you are playing a professional, he will stop worrying about how to win at this point, and start wondering if your check is good, and perhaps how much it's safe to win without your "quitting them" for good.

In every game people want to play someone who "cracks" and "steams." So it must be better not to "crack" or "steam."

One problem is that like many things in golf (such as slicing, hooking, and chipping), the correction is opposite to our natural urge. Our natural urge is to go for a big shot, to "get it all back." The logic that is usually invoked runs along the lines of, "Well, now you're behind after the poor drive, and the miracle shot through the trees is necessary to get you even."

The poker player also feels himself "behind" after losing the big pot and experiences the urge to "get even." The poker player forgets that what is gone is gone, and the only reasonable plan is to maximize our chances from the present forward. Likewise, in order to succeed, the golfer has to learn to live from the present to the future. Trying to get back what is lost leads to disastrously increasing losses. On the tee of the par 4, it is true: Four is what you want to get. But, after that unexpected and unnerving duck hook into the trees, "five is your number." If you try to to get it all back after the duck hook and play all out for a par, you are likely to go for a big number *and* further damage your confidence.

After giving up a shot on a hole, it makes no more sense to go all out for par than it would to start off every hole going all out for birdie. Would you start off on every hole taking any unlikely shot to go all out for birdie or bust? What kind of score would you expect to shoot?

If, after wasting a shot you go all out for par, you are doing the same thing, and you'll get that same high score.

The bad shot is a confidence breaker. But people who go for a big shot after a bad shot don't appreciate the effort "confident" golfers put into building and maintaining confidence. Building confidence merges with "grinding it out," which to a large extent means playing within yourself.

"Playing within yourself" means placing yourself in a statistical position to make rather than miss shots, which means giving yourself shots over and over that can be accomplished a reasonable percentage of the time by a player who plays like you. Your shot selection must take into account both your technical ability *and your state of mind*. Your technical ability and your current state of mind should dictate a choice of shot that you can reasonably expect to make. If your confidence is low, you go for less. If your confidence is high, you go for more. This is a self-correcting formula for success. Since you are always picking a shot you can reasonably expect to make with your current level of confidence, you are always building confidence.

Those who take the other path, of course, are always picking a shot they could not reasonably expect to make with their current level of confidence, so they are always destroying confidence.

If you could use more confidence, plant this idea in your mind: Match your shot choice to your confidence level, and grow your confidence.

16

What's with Visualization?

BY NOW everybody has heard that you are supposed to *visualize* your shot. Then you are supposed to hit it.

But the thoughtless aren't bothering, and the thoughtful are wondering "why bother?"

This raises the question: What is the purpose of this *visualization*? How do you do it, and, most important, is there any actual benefit?

When you visualize a shot, you imagine it, fully, as it is intended to go.

Okay, let's be frank. On the surface this sounds like Pollyanna thinking. So what if I visualize? Suppose I visualize my ball sprouting wings and flying around the moon, and then flying up your nose. Suppose I visualize my ball sprouting wings and flying 400 yards. Will it happen?

The answer is no. No supernatural powers will accrue to your ball no matter what you visualize. But we'll tell you something you may not know.

Now what do you want to do? Every golfer knows the answer to this problem.

A tap-in.

The interesting thing is that this is not the reason why people resist visualizing the shot! People don't resist because doing so fails to impart special powers to the shot. They resist because, in yet another subtle way, people want to cheat. Or, to put it more accurately, people are hungry for applause.

Visualize this: You are fifteen feet off the green with the pin thirty feet past the front edge.

Now what do you want to do? Every golfer knows the answer to this problem.

The problem is that golfers don't know for sure how they are going to arrive at this answer.

But everyone wants credit if the answer is right. There is more than one way to skin a cat, they say. There is certainly more than one way to put the ball near the hole. The Upstairs is saying, "Be careful." The Downstairs is saying, "Hit it." The Ground Floor is balancing these imperatives with the demands of the outside world, including, but not limited to, gravity, green speed, cut recently(?), wet(?), subtle roll, and how the ball is nestling in longer grass.

Certainly the mind imagines a number of good and bad out-

"Telestrator" of bump and roll. (*Photo credit Lee/Chen*)

"Telestrator" of soft lob wedge. (*Photo credit Lee/Chen*)

comes. Generated good outcomes tend to fast-forward through the various early parts of the set of all good shots from here, and instead focus on the final common denominator of all good shots from here: ball close to the hole.

The mind also imagines bad outcomes. Once again the actual shot often is something of a blur, but the bad result—ball rocketed over green, ball duffed a few feet forward—is clearer.

There are two forces that oppose *visualization*, by which we mean the full imagining of one chosen shot from start to finish prior to hitting.

The major force opposing visualization is the desire to take credit for every good outcome.

The mind wants to preen. Part of the Ground Floor wants to "please" the Upstairs by being a star, and the Downstairs is always ready to show off, to "strut our stuff."

Golf is a hard game, and opportunities to strut our stuff do not come along as regularly as we imagined at the outset.

A very hungry person does not care if the roast beef is on the bread (sandwich), or beside the bread (platter). He'll take it any way he can get it.

Similarly, the golfer does not really care if the tap-in gimme got there by air or by parcel post.

In fact, the golfer does not want, even in his own mind, to call his shot. The reason is obvious. The golfer thinks that if the shot is great, he is great (great shot = great golfer). He also thinks if the shot is not great, he is not great. And if he calls it one way and it comes out another, then he is still not great (dog shot = dog golfer).

There are so many ways things can go wrong. No wonder the poor golfer wants credit for all the ways things can go right. It seems only fair.

It is hard enough to put the ball near the hole (one putt distance). The less frequently the ball is in the *good result* area, the stronger the desire to get credit for the (occasional) shot, however it happened.

What are your chances of getting down in two from here?

If your chances are only two in five of chipping the ball into one putt range, then 60 percent of the time you make this chip you are going to be disappointed.

You will not want to further increase the area of disappointment by discounting some good chips just because they didn't go the way you meant, so you won't want to have visualized a specific shot.

So what if it rolls ten feet or twenty feet as long as it ends up in one putt territory? What's the difference? It's close to the hole.

The problem with this is that while trying to take credit for two different outcomes, you will also try to produce two different outcomes.

After all, what is the message being sent to the clubhead? The clubhead can't do the airmail thing and at the same time do the parcel post thing. And the chances of doing either one successfully are greatly diminished unless one single shot path is chosen.

The purpose of visualization is not to put magical wings on the golf ball. The purpose of visualization, in fact, does not have anything at all to do with augmenting the chosen outcome. Rather, it is a formal rejection of other desirable paths.

Visualization is the enabler of commitment. Visualization forces your mind to send one, and only one, set of instructions to the clubhead.

If you don't know how to make the shot on the range, then you won't be able to make the shot on the course, no matter how much you visualize it.

On the range, you tend to send only one set of instructions to the clubhead. If you do know how to make the shot on the range, then visualization, by forcing you to limit yourself to one set of instructions, will facilitate your ability to make the shot on the course.

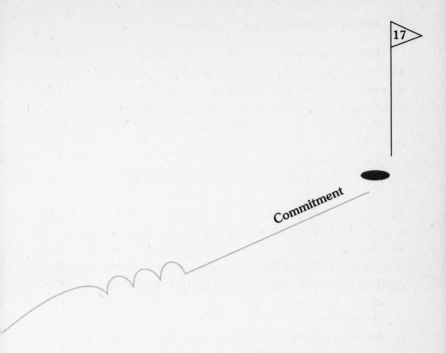

17

Commitment

BACK IN Chapter 2 we discussed the problem facing the golfer with 160 yards over water to a green with the pin on the right guarded by a trap:

The problem is obvious.

The Upstairs says "don't make mistakes." The Basement (caveman) says "go for it!" The Ground Floor wants to be logical and say, "this is 160 yards, let's use our 160-yard club," but the Ground Floor also has to reconcile demands from Upstairs and Downstairs.

The Ground Floor (ourselves) is caught in the middle: It's very hard to go for it and not make mistakes. The more you go for it, the more likely you are to make mistakes. Conversely, the more careful you are not to make mistakes, the less you are going for it. And if you're going to go for it, then it's a full 7. And if you're going to be sure of getting there, it's a 6 iron. And if you're going to go for it, you go over the trap. But if you're going to be sure of getting there, you go for the accessible part of the green. And everybody is watching.

What is the Ground Floor supposed to do?

The Ground Floor is the part of our mind that is accessible, that we think of as us. The Ground Floor (us) is caught in the middle between the impossible to reconcile demands of the Upstairs ("Don't make a mistake!") and the Basement ("Go for it!). What do most golfers do often (and all golfers do sometimes) in this situation?

THE WISDOM(?) OF SOLOMON

Most golfers employ the wisdom of Solomon. They split it in the middle. We'll be half aggressive, half careful. We'll sort of go for it, and kind of not make a mistake. We'll make a conservative club choice (6 iron), but we'll swing a little easier. Or we'll make an aggressive club call (7 iron), but swing a little harder.

We'll aim for center, but maybe we'll fade it for the right-hand pin.

Or we'll aim for the right-hand pin, but we'll favor the draw so if we miss we're still on the green.

What's wrong with this picture?

THERE'S ONLY ONE COLLISION

In all ball-and-stick sports there is only one collision. The bat meets the ball (baseball and cricket). The stick meets the puck (field hockey and ice hockey). The club meets the ball (golf). The face is facing in one direction. It has a determined velocity. And the ball reacts after impact. Only one thing happens.

But golfers are almost unique in that they seem to think they can arrange to have more than one thing happen. This is primarily because golfers have more time to think. Oddly enough, our parents were right: Idle hands are the devil's work.

Mark Messier and Ken Griffey, Jr., are far less likely to try to do two things at once than the average golfer. Ken Griffey, Jr., will not try to hit to left field and to right field at the same time. Mark

Messier will not try to hit the top of the net and the bottom of the net at the same time. But the golfer may try to "go for it" and to "play it safe." Why? Because he has the time to think not only "what do I want to do," but also "what do I not want to do and how can I mystically accomplish both."

More preventable bad shots in golf come from trying to accomplish two things at once than from any other source. The answer to these bad shots is:

COMMITMENT

Commitment sounds almost spiritual. And if not spiritual, then certainly painful. It sounds like a good thing for others. It sounds like you might have to give something up, and in fact you *do* have to give something up, but the good news is you don't have to give up anything that is doing you any good.

Commitment is not about holding your nose and doing something you have already decided you won't do. It's actually not about a particular choice. Commitment is about making one choice at a time.

> PHIL: My office is just off Central Park in Manhattan. If I have a break on a nice spring day, I might decide to go for a walk. On my right is Central Park with the trees coming into bloom. On my left is a place to have lunch. A tough choice. However, I do not walk four steps to the right, then three steps to the left, then five steps to the right, then two steps to the left in some kind of random walk to satisfy both desires. Like everyone else, I know this is a choice: I walk to the park or to the restaurant. Obviously, I know that I cannot do both at once. Obviously, you know that I cannot do both at once.

So why would we both be tempted to try to do two things at once on a golf hole? Part of it is childhood experience. Children have what we call magical thinking; at an early age children are immune to the laws of logic. They think people can be here and there at the same time, they think we can go to the toy store and make dinner. They have no sense of the mutually exclusive. As Freud points out, the appeal of horror and science fiction rests at least in part on our childhood experience with magical thinking, which, especially under duress, is never as far away as we would like to think. Even older children become younger (regress) under pressure from events. After the death of a beloved grandparent:

"Will Grandma come over?"

"I'm sorry, honey, I know you miss her, but remember? Grandma is dead."

"Will she come next week?"

In the face of great hope and fear we all regress a little bit, which means that our thinking—which is never as far from childlike as we would like to think—reverts to the magical. And magical thinking, which in golf usually boils down to accomplishing two things at once, is the enemy of good golf. Putting: I'll hit it hard to be sure I'm not short, but I'll decelerate to be sure I'm not long. Driving: I'll swing through to be sure I don't slice, but I'll lock my wrists to be sure I don't hook.

Visualization is filing one and only one flight plan for the flight of the ball.

Commitment is going all out to accomplish that and only that flight plan.

18

Swing Thoughts

THE NAME itself is misleading. *Thoughts* are what you produce by thinking. *Swings*, as we have seen, are not generally helped by thinking. How many times have you heard someone say after a bad shot "I'm thinking too much"? Conversely, after a career round a player will say, "I was in the zone." If you respond with something like, "Wow, that must be great. What were you thinking about?" the player will invariably look puzzled and say, "Gee, I don't know; I wasn't really thinking about anything. I was just swinging the club."

If there is a correlation between not thinking and good swings, then what is the role of *swing thoughts*? It almost sounds like swing "non-thoughts" are what we are looking for. It almost sounds as if any kind of intentional move toward thinking might be a move in the wrong direction. In other words, if we want to not think, then why would we set out to think? Why would we deliberately embark on a swing *thought*?

That is a good question, and the answer to it begins with another question. What are the alternatives? It is not as though we choose to think or not to think. If you get tired of clapping your hands you can say to yourself, "I'm going to stop clapping my hands now," and the noise will stop. But if you say to yourself, "I'm going to stop thinking now," the noise will not stop.

Based on this true observation that one cannot simply decide to stop thinking, Beard among others has pointed out that the benefit of the swing thought is to exclude other thoughts. The idea here is that any swing thought will help because, whatever the swing thought, it will fill the space in the brain that would otherwise be devoted to either malignant self-criticism or to worries not even related to golf (the marital dispute, the IRS audit, the American Express bill).

In this sense the swing thought has the same role as a cat—for someone who does not particularly like cats—in a house troubled by mice. We don't particularly like the cat, but at least it gets rid of some of the mice.

This theory has some merit. For those who are constantly plagued by self-criticism, and for all the rest who have reached that point in the round where they are *now* the target of an internal investigation, almost any swing thought will displace some of the negative thinking.

But this does not mean that all swing thoughts are equally helpful. In fact this is decidedly not the case. The measure of a swing thought cannot be taken on the printed page. The measure of a swing thought is the extent to which it helps you (and only you) to improve your game.

A swing thought is a very personal thing. If we took a survey and found that we had a swing thought that helped 999 out of 1,000 people, that would not necessarily mean that this was a good swing thought for you.

All through life, and to a large extent all through our golfing life, there is a sense that there's a way to do things and that we need to learn how to adapt ourselves to fit in with that. In golf we see that there are different swings among the pros, but we are correctly reminded that at impact they all look very similar. The message is we better do it like them.

Mercifully, in the world of swing thoughts this is not the case. Another man's shoes may simply not fit. Another man's swing thought—like clothes off the rack—may not work. To be maximally effective a swing thought will be individually tailored to fit your psyche.

People have an intuitive sense that swing thoughts should "fit," but very little idea of the differences between them other than that some fit and others don't. It is somewhat like being in a large department store where all the clothes have been thrown together on one huge table with no size labels. You just put things on, in no particular order, hoping to find something that fits.

This sounds inefficient, and it is. It can also be frustrating. Usually one is trying on a swing thought on the course in a situation where a good swing thought would be helpful. If the swing thought is less than helpful, then results will be disappointing, the player will be frustrated, and there will be even more pressure on the ill-fitting swing thought. This is definitely a vicious circle, and it probably sounds familiar. At this point one of two things happens. You either decide that you weren't "listening" to the swing thought well enough and redouble your efforts to follow the swing thought, or you decide that the swing thought is either no good or used up and you try a new swing thought (or bring out one that previously worked for a while to see if it has somehow gotten its power back).

The implicit analogy, and one that in many ways is helpful, is to the rechargeable nickel cadmium batteries required by portable phones, cameras, and other modern appliances. There are a lot of them that look like they will be good, but most of them don't fit at all. Meanwhile, even if it fits and works, the battery quickly loses its charge, working less and less well and finally dying. Sometimes it can be recharged, at least a certain number of times, before eventually losing its power altogether.

If this sounds familiar in terms of swing thoughts, then the question is how to tell in advance which "battery" will fit, and how to make the "charge" last as long as possible at an effective level. Are there some simple rules for swing thought construction so that we can be reasonably sure we are carrying a swing thought to the course that will perform when we need it?

The first rule of medicine is said to be *non nocere*, which is Latin for "do no harm." The first rule of swing thought construction is likewise to do no harm. This is just common sense—the first rule in trying to make things better is not to make them worse. There is nothing that does more harm, particularly under pressure, than negative swing thoughts.

▶ RULE 1. NO NEGATIVE SWING THOUGHTS.

What is a negative swing thought? This is a swing thought that tells you *not* to do something. Typically, this swing thought begins with the word DON'T. Some common examples would be:

> Don't look up.
> Don't come over the top.
> Don't cast.
> Don't get quick.
> Don't hit it fat.
> Don't thin it.
> Don't shank it.
> Don't blade it.

Freud said that there are no *negatives* in the subconscious. The body is not wired well for negative instructions. It is important to understand the problem, which is simply this: If you say to your right forefinger, "Touch my right ear," then you will have no problem. Of course your right forefinger will touch your right ear.

But if you issue the command to your right forefinger, "Don't touch my right ear," there will be a bit of minor confusion.

The body will not know if you mean to *activate* the muscles that push your right forefinger away from your ear, or whether you mean to *deactivate* the muscles that brought your right forefinger up to your ear in the first place.

For every motion your body can accomplish, there are two ways not to do it. If you tell your body *not* to putt too hard, then there are two things your body can do. It can try to turn down the muscles that are making the putt go too far, or it can turn up the muscles that would make the putter go in the other direction.

If this sounds reasonable but confusing to you, imagine how it sounds to your body. Your body never went to school. Your body is just doing the best it can, based on training and experience, to do what you tell it to do.

If you tell your body not to do something, it will do its best. It will, to some extent, deactivate the muscles that cause that action; and it will, to some extent, activate the muscles that oppose that action.

Of course, when you say to your body, "Don't knock it past the hole," you have one specific idea in mind. You want the ball close to the hole.

But when you activate two opposing sets of muscles, what you get is an extra layer of inconsistency: You get the inconsistency of the set of muscles pushing the ball toward the hole plus the inconsistency of the set of muscles pulling back in order to slow the club.

In short, it is better to give one and only one set of instructions to the muscles. Never tell the body not to do something.

▶ **RULE 2. YOU CAN PLAY *SIMON SAYS* BUT REMEMBER IT'S ONLY A GAME.**

What is *Simon Says*? Well, you remember how to play:

Simon Says take one step forward.
Simon Says take one step backward.

Simon Says turn to the left.
Simon Says touch your chin with your shoulder.
Finish with your hands high. Wait! I didn't say *Simon Says*!

The *Simon Says* swing thoughts are the most common thoughts, and they are helpful especially when learning new material. *Simon Says* swing thoughts are direct commands to the body to do things. Some common examples would be: (*Simon Says*)

> Keep the left arm straight.
> (Take it away) low and slow.
> Complete the backswing.
> Follow through.
> Finish with the hands high.
> Turn to face the target.
> Shift before turning.
> Keep the right elbow in.
> Keep the head down (back, still) through impact.

The disadvantage of *Simon Says* swing thoughts is that they tend to wear out quickly and to break down under pressure.

These are usually somewhat helpful initially because they express general truths about better swings. However, if they are initially helpful, then that means that these general truths were not present in your swing at the time you adopted the swing thought.

One interesting note on the breakdown rate of the *Simon Says* swing thoughts is that it correlates with the extent to which the *Simon Says* thought is actually a disguised negative thought. "Don't bend your left arm" can become "keep the left arm straight," just as "don't let your right elbow fly out" can become "keep the right elbow in." "Don't get fast" can masquerade as "low and slow." But you won't fool yourself, and a disguised negative swing thought will cause as much trouble as a straightforward negative swing thought.

However, truly positive *Simon Says* swing thoughts are easily constructed and generally helpful, but have a short half-life.

One wonders if there is a formula for a more helpful swing thought. How would one construct a powerful swing thought?

▶ **RULE 3. PLAY CHARADES.**

Powerful swing thoughts use actions you already know how to perform as their building blocks.

You want physical activities that you can act out and communicate, at least to someone exactly like you. Suppose you had an identical twin who also shared every experience you have had since birth. Or suppose that you had somehow just been cloned, so that there were two identical *you*s. Now imagine that you can't speak, but you need to communicate to your clone or twin that you need a hammer. Imagine the hammering motion you make, wrist and forearm flexing rhythmically, then mimicking impact with the nail. Even if you have never used a hammer in your life (and never had a lesson from a PHA—Professional Hammer Association—professional), still you can recognize, perform, and repeat these motions.

If you want the saltshaker but your mouth is full (and no one is there but your clone, so manners don't matter), then you will make the universal salt-shaking motion with your hand and forearm and you will be understood. If you need a toothbrush in a foreign country, you can enter a pharmacy, bare your teeth, and do the universal tooth-brushing motion and be understood.

These kinds of physical motions, and there are more of them than you think, are the basic building blocks of effective swing thoughts. You don't actually need to postulate a clone: Anyone can understand them. What charade thoughts have in common is that you can perform them repeatedly without any mental rehearsal, they have nothing to do with golf, and they contain an inner rhythm of their own. The latter is perhaps the most important feature.

WE CAN THINK OF INCORPORATING ONE OF THESE MOVEMENTS
AS INSTALLING A "RHYTHM CHIP."

Try it right now: Put down this page and perform a charade of brushing your teeth, of shaking salt on your food, of hammering a nail.

The interesting thing you discover is that there is a certain rate at which you perform the motions. You don't "shake the salt" or "brush the teeth" any slower or any faster, even though you could. Try, if you will, speeding up and then slowing down the motions. You can do it easily, but it doesn't "feel right." And "feel" is the important word; you don't have to think about it. Tomorrow, and next week, and next month, you could say to yourself, "I'm going to do that tooth brushing motion," and it would be performed at the same rate without any counting or other effort. The hammer motion and the salt-pouring motion could be videotaped, and they would look the same and take almost identical amounts of time to perform. It is quite surprising, when you stop to think about it, that if you wore the same clothes in front of the same background you would need quite sophisticated electronic equipment to detect any difference at all between the various recordings of "salt-shaking," "tooth-brushing," or "hammering."

The idea of installing some kind of rhythm regulator or governor in the golf swing seems intuitively desirable. How often do we see a practice swing that even resembles the actual swing? How often does our putting rhythm on the practice green feel like our putting rhythm under pressure? And isn't that also sometimes true in the sand, over water, or on the tee?

By linking elements of the golf swing to activities that contain a built-in rhythm, we can dampen the variations in rhythm that are caused by anxiety. Ledbetter and others have pointed out the importance of repeatability in the swing; proper mental linkage with repeatable activities will make the swing more repeatable.

▶ RULE 4. ADVANCED SWING THOUGHTS

The Rifleman

You don't have to be old enough to remember Chuck Connors in the TV western series as the man so good with a rifle that he didn't need a pistol, you can still benefit mightily from this swing thought.

Golfers who are blocking their shots will benefit from this swing thought. Think of the club as a shotgun.

Players know that the left arm must fold and pronate after impact. However, trying to make the left arm do this can be frustrating. Training aids may attempt to hold the upper part of the left arm after impact (harness-type aids), or may put something (club cover, towel) in the left armpit where the idea is not to drop the object by not letting the left arm move out from the side of the chest after impact.

However, there is a simple swing thought that can free the natural pronation of the left arm. An additional benefit is that the swing thought contains no negative instructions that will induce one set of muscles to fight against another set of muscles: In the club-cover exercise, the muscles that hold the club cover under the arm are instructed to overpower the muscles that are pushing the left arm out from the body after impact. It is easy to see that this kind of resolution is unlikely to hold up over time, and will certainly explode under stress.

Think of the club as a shotgun. (*Photo credit Steve Dolce*)

In this swing thought there is a "bad guy" directly behind you on the swing plane line. You "cover" the bad guy by pointing the shotgun directly at him in the backswing. (*Photo credit Steve Dolce*)

However, there is a second bad guy who is about to pop up in front of you on the intended line of flight of the ball. (*Photo credit Steve Dolce*)

In the ¾ follow-through position, the gun points directly at the bad guy in front. (*Photo credit Steve Dolce*)

Note that in the finish position, the gun points directly at the head-on observer. (*Photo credit Steve Dolce*)

WHY DOES THIS SWING THOUGHT WORK?

Like all good swing thoughts, this one draws upon a knowledge and a rhythm that we already possess.

You have only to pick up a toy rifle, or a stick, or even a golf club held backward with the grip as the end of the barrel. Pretend to point it at something as in the picture on page 167.

Notice then how your left arm has pronated and folded all by itself!

This move, which can be so frustrating and difficult to make by conscious effort, happens all by itself.

We have all tried to just "let it happen," but the question has been what to do when it doesn't just happen. The answer is to find a way of thinking that untangles the messages to the body. There is no need to reinvent the wheel. The program for pronation is already

A swing thought for completing the swing is then, of course, to point the gun at the head-on observer. (*Photo credit Steve Dolce*)

written in our brains; this swing thought is a way to access that program.

When we try to make our hands or arms do something that they aren't doing, we get into trouble. When we think about pointing a gun down the target line, our hand and arm pronate automatically. Try it.

The Little Girl

The over-the-top move is a sometime problem for the amateur, and an occasional problem for the more advanced player under pressure. All remedies involve getting the left hip to move, and the weight to shift, before firing the right side.

But it is hard to tell individual parts of the body what to do. Once again, it is far more efficient and successful to find a code for something the body knows how to do already.

The mischievous little boy is about to cut in front of your shy little girl to steal her loot bag at the birthday party. Since his mother is watching, you have to be subtle. (*Photo credit Steve Dolce*)

Your hips just happen to block his path as you guide your little girl through to the loot table. It all happens so smoothly and naturally you could easily claim you didn't even know he was there. (*Photo credit Steve Dolce*)

At the moment of impact, the right palm moves straight down the line toward the loot table. Clearly, there will be no sudden movement of the hand to the inside (hook or save), as this will throw the little girl into the bad boy. Nor, of course, will the right hand push the little girl out into the foreground banister (weak push). (*Photo credit Steve Dolce*)

Relaxed follow-through with the pace of the little girl leading the hand (club pulling the arms into the finish). Note that with a more complete weight shift, the bad boy would be even more effectively screened from the play. (*Photo credit Steve Dolce*)

In this swing thought we are trying to usher our little girl forward to the loot table at a birthday party. Unfortunately, some bad little boy keeps cutting in front of the little girl and taking all the goodies.

Complicating the situation is the fact that the mother of the bad boy is watching us with an eagle eye.

We must be subtle in blocking him out while shepherding our little girl directly forward toward the goodies. (Of course, we can't hurry her lest she trip or mutiny; she sets her own pace.)

Swing thoughts are not an end in themselves

The power of a swing thought can be measured by its ability to dominate our thinking, at least to the point where we no longer need it, because—do not forget, do not be confused—a swing thought is a means to an end, a taxi to the airport. And when we say *a means to an end*, the end point we have in mind is not a good swing: The end point is the end of thinking.

Swing thoughts facilitate movement in a particular direction, and that movement is in the direction of *the zone*. The closer we get to the zone, the less we need the swing thought. A good swing thought, like a good swing doctor, eventually makes itself obsolete.

19

Fast Fix—The Driver

MANY PEOPLE have more trouble with the driver than with any other club. This is often attributed to the extra length of the "big stick." While this extra length is a factor, there are at least two compensating factors: The ball is hit off of a tee, and the head of the driver ranges from large to huge (in the modern titanium format). But even with these compensations the driver can be surprisingly difficult to hit well, especially on the course.

Those who have read to this point in the book know already that if something is especially difficult to do *on the course* as opposed to *on the range*, that means there is a psychological component.

In addition to the anxieties and pressures already discussed, there is a peculiarity of the driver not shared by any other club that can be an unrecognized psychological-physical problem. When we say *unrecognized*, we mean something distinct from the pressure caused by a hazard on the left or right or the anxiety of performing in a situation in which one feels pressure. These are all recognized anxieties: We feel the pressure.

The unrecognized anxiety of the driver comes from the other difference between that club and all others: With all other clubs there is known distance that we wish to achieve. More to the point *there is a known distance that would constitute too much*. A 7 iron hit over the green is not good.

With the driver we often do not have this desire not to go too far, and this brings its own special problems, which can be expressed very simply.

Some parts of the mind/body will want to hit far, and some parts of the mind/body will want to hit safely. The discrepancy between these two desires, being unrecognized, is also unresolved.

Either one can be a worthy objective. Trying to do both at once is a mental error that leads to inconsistency, awkwardness, poor shot-making, and loss of confidence.

This is a mental error that masquerades as a physical error, and does so convincingly enough that many players are completely taken in. It can have the unfortunate consequence of inducing a player to change a perfectly good swing.

A player might, for instance, regularly drive 230 yards with reasonable accuracy, and the same player might be able to drive 270 yards if he goes all out—with an increased chance for missing the fairway, of course. But if he activates both swings at once, his chances of error are enormously compounded, so much so that he may be misled into trying to change his swing rather than his mind.

Driver problems with significant hazards on the right and on the left have been discussed in Tiger on the Right and Tiger on the Left. But if you are having problems with the driver in general on the course but not on the range, then this deceptively simple exercise is for you.

Eliminate the Basement exercise

What is going on: The Upstairs is saying "be careful." The Basement is saying "go for it." The two demands are incompatible, and your body is caught in the squeeze. Your muscles are getting two sets of commands, and some are following one set while some are following the other. It's amazing that you are doing as well as you are doing!

What the exercise does: The object of the exercise is to eliminate one of the two sets of commands.

What to do: The next time you tee off, treat the driver like an iron. No, we don't mean to change your swing, not at all. We mean pick out an area on the fairway that you would reasonably expect to hit if that area were the green of a par 3. To make this exercise work, that "green" should be well within your average driving distance. When you pick a 7 iron to hit a green, you feel that an average 7 iron will reach the green, then you worry about direction. In this exercise, you imagine a green where an average drive will easily reach the green, then you line up for direction.

Evaluation: It is of paramount importance to imagine a green where going off the back is death. The one thing you do not want to be in this exercise is long. Left, right, and short all leave chances for recovery, but long is lost. Every time you aren't long in this exercise you are a winner.

Advanced exercise—eliminate the Upstairs

When you have mastered the above exercise you will probably be scoring better. If that is good enough for you, then your driving problem is solved. If you want more, then do this simple exercise. But you have to have the stomach for it.

What is going on: In the above exercise, you have minimized the role of the Basement. You have maximized the role of the Upstairs ("don't make a mistake") by focusing simply on hitting a target.

What this exercise does: This exercise minimizes the role of the Upstairs, while maximizing the role of the Basement.

What you do: You pick a particular distance from the tee box that would constitute a "good" drive for you. Not a "career" drive, but a good drive. By this we mean a distance that, if you were swinging freely, you could expect to hit the ball 50 percent of the time. This should be close to average driving-range distance for you. Now imagine a circle with your average driving-range distance as the radius drawn around the tee box. Line up properly, but then (and yes, this is the hard part) erase the golf course from your internal computer screen. Forget the traps, forget the trees, forget the water, even forget the fairway. You are on a range, or on the edge of the ocean. Then hit the ball beyond the circumference of the circle.

Evaluation: Any shot that goes beyond the circumference of the circle (beyond average driving-range distance) is a winner. Any shot short of the circle (fairway or not) is a loser. You may want to play this game alone at first, but as you get into it you will eliminate hazard fear. When you can keep this and only this score, you will have eliminated hazard fear.

Alternate between these two exercises until you can switch back and forth at will. Previously, the Upstairs ("don't mess up!") and the Basement ("go for it!") would both shout in your backswing, sending two conflicting commands that added up to the destruction of your range game.

When you can switch back and forth between these two exercises like channels on a TV set, then you are able to use one appropriate set of commands at a time. You will have eliminated a source of internal conflict, eliminated a set of conflicting demands on your golf swing.

During your backswing there will be only one voice, only one set of commands for your muscles. They will be greatly relieved. And so will you, because on the tee you will be contemplating something so much more like your range game.

20

First Tee Anxiety

LET US proceed to the first tee. To paraphrase what Kelsey said about a different game over twenty years ago, this is a very exciting moment. No mistakes have yet been made. All things are still possible.

But how many people regard the first tee in this way?

For many people, the experience of going to the first tee falls somewhere between a job interview and an IRS examination. If the saber-toothed tiger roams through tunnels beneath the course like some guerrilla ready to spring up at the most unexpected moment, then the lair of the saber-toothed tiger often seems to be the first tee.

It is interesting to contemplate why that is. There's the obvious fact that at the first tee other people are gathered and one is under some scrutiny. But why is this generally worse at the first tee than it is subsequently? There are several important reasons.

Stranger anxiety is built into all human beings. We are all hardwired to be frightened of strangers. Every ten-month-old baby will smile at the sight of its mother and cry at the sight of a stranger. As we grow up we grow away from this, but more slowly and painfully than we remember. We were all more or less afraid of baby-sitters, afraid to go to nursery school, afraid to go to kindergarten, afraid to go to first grade, nervous about new classes and changes of schools, anxious about new jobs and concerned about new dates, and so on. These concerns grow out of an inbred fear of strangers, which we inherit from the caveman as surely as we inherit the fear of the saber-toothed tiger. There may have been little children in the cave who were not afraid of strangers, but they did not grow up to have many children of their own. We are all descended from the cavepeople who were afraid of both strangers and saber-toothed tigers. We carry this fear with us right onto the first tee.

There's no place more closely associated with playing in front of strangers than the first tee. Even when playing in a foursome of complete strangers, they are necessarily more completely strangers on the first tee than at any other time. The better we know the people we're playing with, the less uncomfortable we are on the first tee. Nonetheless, even with those we know well, the first tee will be slightly more anxiety-provoking than those that follow it. This is because there's always a process of *refreshment* in terms of our comfort level with those we know: It can take a few holes for the full level of comfort to be restored. There is a subliminal (from the Upstairs) expectation that even those we know well will not accept us if we don't perform well. Obviously this is a learned as well as an inherited trait, since those who knew us best (our parents) gave us the impression at an early age that they did not accept us if we did not perform well.

The first tee is also anxiety-provoking because of the process known as *generalization*. This is an extremely important principle from the field of behavior therapy. If you have a phobia about dogs and you see a dog on Forty-second Street, you will have a panic attack. You'll be very frightened and very anxious. There's nothing surprising about that because, after all, you do have a phobia about dogs. Subsequently, however, when you are on Forty-second Street, although there is no dog, you may have another panic attack. The stimulus for anxiety (dogs) will generalize to a location where you have seen dogs. Many people have been anxious in the past on the first tee, and sometimes that anxiety generalizes to the first tee itself. (The same process applies to sand and to water: After you've been anxious enough times at particular sand traps or at particular water hazards, sand traps or water hazards themselves may provoke anxiety.)

Another reason people are anxious on the first tee is *superstition*. On some level many people feel that if they start off well it is going to be a good day, and conversely that if they start poorly it is going to be a bad day. Of course, this is a self-fulfilling prophecy.

The first tee can also provoke anxiety due to what we call *competitive comfort level*. People come to the golf course with the often unconscious fear that they will perform poorly, that they will disappoint, and even that they will be the subject of unspoken ridicule. In the mental world, others are going to perform well and you're going to perform badly. After a number of holes in the usual round of golf, two things have happened to deflate this grim fantasy. Hopefully you will have hit enough good shots that you feel you have some "money in the bank." This refers to the internal sense that you can now afford to make a mistake. The feeling is that one has to establish one's worth. Once the golfer has hit a number of good shots, he feels that a bad shot is looked upon more as an aberration, an exceptional event that does not represent him. On the first tee, with no money in the bank, the golfer is under the greatest pressure he will feel for the entire round. Since there are no good shots already established, he will be judged entirely by the shot he is about to make. In a similar manner, but to a lesser degree, the drive is under pressure on every hole, though the pressure is somewhat less once one has already hit some good drives.

The other thing that usually happens to help establish a competitive comfort level after several holes is that one or more of the other players has usually hit some bad shots. It is not immediately apparent why this should make us more comfortable with our own

game, but everybody knows that in some way it does. Our own Upstairs is a critical boss, and we project this sense of judgment and
criticism out onto others. We imagine that they're viewing us in one
of the ways that we view ourselves. We imagine that they are standing on high looking down upon us and judging us. After they hit a
few bad shots, we belatedly realize that they are not perfect people
who are judging our imperfections (our early view of our parents).

It's almost a relief to realize that part of the pleasure we take in
the poor shots of others has nothing to do with delighting in their
misery and everything to do with removing them from the *higher
than us* and *looking down on us* position that we have imagined them
to occupy.

We come to the course dreaming that the other people are looking down on us and judging us, and a few bad shots from them help
us to awaken from this bad dream.

After a few rereadings of this chapter you should be able to awaken
from this nightmare before you get to the first tee.

Your playing partners may still be sleepwalking for a few holes.
Which is too bad for them, but at least you have woken up. Isn't it
amazing how much less threatening those bad dreams are in the light
of day?

21

Alignment and Target Awareness

WHEN WE see students warming up or practicing on the range, we routinely ask them what their target is. The two most common responses are:

1. "Straight out." It is not easy to say exactly what this means.
2. "I'm not aiming, I'm just working on my swing."

To improve at golf, it is important to always have a definite target both in practice and on the course. It is critical for the developing player to recognize that the ball itself is not the target, but rather is something that is swung through toward a distant, specific target. Without a target the swing cannot be instinctive or athletic.

Once a player has identified his target line, it is critical that he align properly. If the player is misaligned, he will make subconscious adjustments to get the ball to his target.

There are many transient "swing flaws" that are caused by misaligning—consciously or unconsciously—with the target.

Normal misalignment comes from a history of missing the ball in a certain direction (most slicers aim left, most hookers aim right).

However, many players just don't aim consistently in either direction, and are further thrown off by fear of hazards (see Chapters 10 and 11) or poorly aligned tee markers, or overfocus on the ball rather than the target. Additionally, many poor aimers say they just can't line properly because of poor optics: "It looks to me like I am lined up right; there must be something wrong with my eyes." Of course, this is a fallacy.

Another common fallacy is that alignment problems can be cured by picking an intermediate target close to you, say a piece of grass two to six feet in front of your ball. This strategy was popularized by Jack Nicklaus; obviously it worked for him, and can be helpful.

But it is not a cure-all. When poor aimers use this method they end up as far off as—or more than—usual because they never look up to their actual target. They are just as many degrees off at six feet as they are at 150 yards. A two-inch error at six feet equals a huge error at 200 yards.

Go to any professional tournament and observe the players on the range. Almost always, at some point in their practice, they have their caddies behind them lining them up and/or have alignment clubs on the ground. Notice also how they take frequent long looks at the target, and short glances at the ball. The target is their focus—the ball is merely a point through which the club travels.

To promote proper alignment skills and an athletic repetitive swing:

1. Lay down a club through the ball pointing out to your target.
2. Lay a second club down parallel to that for your stance and body lines.

3. Take care to aim the clubface carefully at your target and parallel to your stance and body lines.

4. Position your feet, knees, hips, shoulders, and eyes parallel to the target line.

5. Take several looks down the target line—**if it looks odd to you then you have an alignment problem.** Repeat this process daily both at the golf course and at home until your eyes see what "straight" really is.

6. Finally, remove the club on your target line and hit balls—staring frequently at the target.

(*Photo credit Phil Lee*)

Remember, if your eyes can believe your former alignment (as much as fifty yards off in certain cases) was right, then it shouldn't take long for them to accept what is actually correct.

MIND-BODY NOTE Continue this drill in the off-season indoors and every time you practice. Your aiming skills will improve dramatically. Of course, there was never anything wrong with your "optics"—your eyes have just not been trained properly.

Finally, when you practice and play have your routine include two to three intense stares at the target with mere glances at the ball.

MENTAL MASTERNOTE Making the target your priority and the ball merely a detail will free you to swing athletically, powerfully, and efficiently.

22

How to Hit More Greens Without Changing Your Swing

JEFF: I once had the experience at a charity event of playing a 150-yard par 3 with every group in a one-hundred-player field composed mainly of medium-high handicap golfers. The hole played over a gorge and deep bunkers and the ball had to be carried 135 yards to reach a generous putting surface. Nearly every group asked me the yardage, threw some grass around, and appeared to have some procedure for pulling the proper club.

A common part of that procedure was to ask one of their playing partners questions like "Do you think I can get there with a 7 iron?"

Sixteen people reached the green that day. Two skulled it over, six were even with the green but missed left or right. That left seventy-six balls short of a 135-yard carry, much less than the 150 yards required to reach the hole.

After watching this unfold, I wondered how the results would have been different if every player had hit one more club (for instance, a 6 iron instead of a 7). This may sound like negative thinking, but even the best players in the world hit the ball exactly perfect only 10 percent of the time.

The difference is they calculate this into their club selection. The average players seem to choose a club that would only reach the flag under perfect conditions with a perfect shot.

I had worked with and watched most of these players warm up on the range that morning. During that time I saw very little to rationally justify the club selections I was seeing on the course.

MIND-BODY NOTE   There are several reasons why players commonly take too little club.

1. Competitiveness: It's all about who hit what, isn't it? "What did you hit? 7 iron? Really! I hit a wedge."
2. Ignorance (or trying to fit in): "Why did I hit a 7? I don't know, that's what my friends hit."
3. Age: "I've been using a 7 iron from 150 yards since before you were born."
4. Arrogance: "I just didn't get all of it. I know exactly how far my 7 iron goes." Translation: "Once when I was in Colorado at 7,000 feet hitting downhill from a wet grassy (flyer) lie downwind on hard ground, I had a 7 iron go 150 yards. And therefore, by the way, my 6 iron goes 160 yards and so on down to my 2 iron, which must go 200 yards—except my driver goes that far."

There is obviously something wrong with these figures. And who pays the price of these illusory calculations? If you are the one miscalculating, then you are also the one picking up the tab. That's okay, you can charge it to your handicap. Or you can fix the problem fast, and at the same time perform a fast fix on your handicap.

Bill thinks he hits his 7 iron 150 yards. He does, two times out of ten, and you can see them beside the pin. But because his average distance is 143 yards he has left himself difficult shots. (If there is a trap in front of the green, the shots will look even more difficult.) (*Photo credit Phil Lee*)

Bill can hit his 6 iron 152 yards on average. Obviously, he is in a better position to score more often. (*Photo credit Phil Lee*)

Fast fix

To find out how far you realistically and consistently hit the ball, find a spot where you can hit ten balls with each club in your bag. Have someone chart where these balls land. (Note: Choose a windless day, use good balls, and find a level area.)

Don't count your best shots as your "normal" distance with each club. Try to find the yardage with each club that the most balls went. This means your dead flush shots should finish beyond the target.

Mental Note This means you will have an opportunity to make birdies on your less-than-perfect shots as well as on your good ones.

As you develop these charts to determine your mean yardage with each club, you become aware of specific strengths and weaknesses in your game.

If you are unhappy with your grid results—or the frequency of solid shots—then improve your mechanical ability through practice or a mechanical adjustment.

Meanwhile, lower your scores with a dose of reality and statistical probability without any swing change whatsoever!

Glendower: "I can summon spirits from the vasty deep!"

Hotspur: "Why, so can I, or so can any man. But will they come?"

ALTHOUGH SHAKESPEARE had the misfortune to be born before golf was invented, he nonetheless seems to have understood some important things about the pre-shot routine.

The purpose of the pre-shot routine is indeed to summon spirits from the vasty deep, to mystically enhance our ability to perform.

But while anyone can perform some sort of pre-shot routine, the question always is "but will they come?" Will some added benefit be conferred upon our game as a result of our pre-shot efforts?

This is not a rhetorical question. The answer is yes, a good pre-shot routine is quite helpful. The question for most golfers, though, is what constitutes a "good" pre-shot routine?

Ask one hundred golfers what a pre-shot routine is and you will get two main answers. One answer is that it is something you do the same way before each shot, and the other answer is that it is something to do with lining up the shot.

Both answers are correct as far as they go, but we need to go farther. If you follow up with "why do you do these things," you will get the honest "I dunno," the reasonable "well, it's important to line up," or the historically accurate "it's what people say to do."

It shows the power of the pre-shot routine that, with so little understanding of its nature and purpose, so many people are able to extract some benefit from it some of the time.

A thorough understanding of the nature and purpose of the pre-shot routine will enable you to extract a more powerful benefit from it more often.

"But will they come?"

They will, if your pre-shot routine is effective.

WHAT IS THE PRE-SHOT ROUTINE?

The pre-shot routine is not peculiar to golf. Such a routine is found in all sports at the highest level. It may be associated with golf in the minds of most readers of this book, but the pre-shot routine is more accurately associated with success in golf and other sports.

When Ivan Lendl was the number one tennis player in the world, he used to bounce the ball before he served. Of course, everyone knows and does that. But he himself made the point that he bounced the ball four times before his first serve, and three times before his second serve. Always. Without variation. Always four times before the first, always three times before the second.

That is a pre-shot routine.

Watch an outstanding major league hitter. You will almost always see the same pattern of practice swings in the on-deck circle, the same method of setting stance in the batter's box, the same final routine of practice swings in the batter's box before the assumption of the same stance. If you watch other details of players with more elaborate pre-shot routines, you will see exact repetition there, too.

Watch the order and sequence of Chuck Knoblauch donning the batting gloves. The ceremony is as exact and precise as something one might see in a church.

A professional free-throw shooter in the NBA will assume the same stance in the same way, bounce the ball identically, grip, look, breathe, and deliver with the same motion and rhythm on every free throw. This is another pre-shot routine.

At first glance, certainly in golf and to a lesser extent in these other sports, the purpose appears to be to line up. But this is deceptive.

The true purpose is to go through a ritualized series of steps in order to induce a "focused," almost trancelike state in which concentration and relaxed attention are focused on the task at hand. Extraneous thoughts are expelled by the pre-shot routine; a previously achieved level of calm attention to the task at hand is summoned from "the vasty deep" of past experience.

The pre-shot routine is an informal signal to the body and mind to approach "the zone" of relaxed attention and effortless performance.

It isn't actually necessary to bounce a tennis ball before serving it, but a few repeated steps obviously and intuitively make it easier to focus on the ball and establish a rhythm. For this reason very few tennis players serve without bouncing the ball first, and those who do also have some rhythm of rocking and of moving the ball and racket together prior to serving, which performs the same function.

In baseball, it is clearly more difficult to pitch when there are men on base. But it isn't only the distraction of having men on base that makes it harder to pitch in that situation, nor is it entirely the need to deliver the ball more quickly so as not to give the base runner time to steal, though both of these are added difficulties.

Pitching "more suddenly," even without men on base, would be more difficult because the pre-shot routine of the windup is being sacrificed. Without a set routine to induce rhythm and focus it is marginally more difficult to pitch accurately, and in all these sports a little difference counts for a lot.

There is not that much physical difference between a fly ball to the warning track and a home run, but over the course of a season these differences add up. There isn't that much difference between a ball hit squarely 180 yards to the front of the green and a ball hit a couple grooves off 175 yards into the water, or between a putt that lips out and one that is center cut. But it doesn't take a whole season, or even a whole round, for the differences to build.

A good pre-shot routine may not put us in the zone, but if it puts us even marginally closer to the zone we will see tangible improvements.

One of the things we are most commonly asked about is the relationship between the pre-shot routine and lining up. Obviously, there is a relationship inasmuch as most golfers line up as part of their pre-shot routine. However, the relationship is one of convenience rather than necessity.

It is clearly necessary to line up your shot. If you were the most focused golfer who ever lived, if you had the repetitive accuracy of a gun or of Iron Byron (the mechanical striking device used by the USGA to test golf balls), you would still need to be aimed toward the target in order to hit it.

It is also necessary to have a series of focus-inducing steps that can be repeated in all shot-making circumstances prior to the shot. The psychological purpose of these motions is analogous to the after-dinner speaker who rises, taps on a water glass with the silverware, and then clears his throat. As he sends out these signals, the many voices in the room quiet over several seconds, and attention shifts to the speaker. This is what the pre-shot routine does: It quiets the many voices in our head, and directs our attention to the upcoming event.

It is necessary literally to quiet the voices in our head and focus a calm, quiet, expectant attention on the upcoming shot. Otherwise we end up like the golfer who is muttering to himself "just keep your head down (you jerk)" or "follow through for once, will you?" We have all seen or been that golfer, and we all know the next shot is not likely to work out any better than the last. That golfer has not quieted the room. The Upstairs and the Downstairs are cajoling, criticizing, and demanding. That golfer has little chance of satisfying the various demands, of silencing the clamoring of the room. His ability (his range game) is not free to operate; it is under attack from the various voices in the room saying such things as "Don't go in the water," "Don't hook it," "Don't screw up!" With all that noise, even if "follow through" happens to be good advice, it will not be heard.

Since it is necessary to line up the shot, and since it is necessary (as we will see in the next section) to have a brief physical ritual to signal for quiet in the room between our ears, it makes sense to utilize portions of lining up in our pre-shot routine. There are two good reasons for this.

First of all, it saves time. If we need to do three things to line up, and if we need to do three things to quiet the room, then it makes sense to do the same three things. This saves our and everyone else's time on the golf course since we are doing three things rather than six before each shot.

The second reason we mesh the line-up and the pre-shot routine is even more powerful. At the end of the line-up, we are in a physical position to hit; it is at precisely this point in time that we need to be psychologically in a position to hit as well. Focus is fragile and does not travel well. Ivan Lendl would not bounce the ball four times in the dressing room then go out and serve, because it wouldn't help. The after-dinner speaker could bang on the glass and clear his throat before anyone showed up for dinner or, less absurdly, five minutes before he was about to speak, but it wouldn't work. The hush is transitory and depends upon the next action (speaking or hitting) filling the brief attention void.

That is the real reason why setting up is, to some extent, incorporated in the pre-shot routine of all the sports. The free-throw shooter, the batter, the server, the golfer achieve a brief and crucially helpful narrowing of focus just prior to the shot, which is utilized at that precise point or lost forever.[1]

---

[1]The stammerer and the stutterer fear that moment when the echo of the silver on the water glass dies away, knowing that if they can just get started at this point things

POWERING UP THE PRE-SHOT ROUTINE

The pre-shot routine gets its power from its ability to allow the golfer to enter what, for lack of a better term, we call a light trance state. It is an attempt to approximate a naturally occurring trance state that is commonly referred to as "the zone."

The act of entering the light trance state could be called self-hypnosis. We call it the **zone-move**. It has many other names, and there are countless methods for achieving it. Other names include guided imagery, autogenics, relaxation exercises, meditation, sometimes even yoga.

WHAT IS THE *ZONE-MOVE*?

Have you ever been driving along in a car and suddenly realized that for the past several miles you hadn't been paying attention to the road? This is a state of self-hypnosis or trance that we can appropriate. And notice how well things work out. You are in a trance state—or, if you prefer, simply "daydreaming"—and yet the car is driven along perfectly well, stays in its lane, and doesn't hit anything.

But driven perfectly well by whom, one may wonder. Since your thoughts and attention are elsewhere, who is driving the car? Obviously, you are driving the car, but in a different state of mind than usual. One difference will be that you have no memory of the drive or of anything that you passed. It is as if your eyes were focused inward; often one has a visual memory of the daydream, as if one were watching television during the drive. But apparently another part of our mind is capable of using our eyes, and of getting our hands and feet to perform the complicated task of running a heavy

---

will go relatively well, but fearing that they will not get started. Similarly, there are golfers who complete the pre-shot routine and then freeze over the ball, despite having promised themselves that this time it won't happen (again).

automobile at high speed on a highway—all "without our knowl-edge."

There are two ways to react to this set of events. One is to be frightened that we sat in a hurtling automobile with "no one" driv-ing. However, we don't know that this is a logical concern, because it is quite possible, and we daresay likely, that far more accidents occur in a normal state than in a trance state. We don't actually know if any accidents have occurred in this trance state.

The other way to react to the news that one can perform a complicated physical task while paying no conscious attention is to marvel at a new opportunity. The specific opportunity to which we refer is the opportunity to do a complicated physical task (hit a golf ball) with the part of the mind that has done such a nice job of driving our car. Of course, this means that we get to use less of that other part of our mind that registers and responds to those score-killers such as pressure, hope, fear, and competitiveness.

Has the light ever changed from red to green without you real-izing it right away, or without you realizing it until someone honks? That also is the same trance state; that is all that self-hypnosis is. Daydreaming in a lecture or a meeting or during a conversation is this same light trance state. So we see there is nothing very unusual or remarkable about this state. Most people enter it often enough, and if it is helpful to be able to enter it for playing golf, especially in pressure situations, then there is no problem with that. Or is there?

The problem is that while this trance or "daydreaming" state is common enough, there is still something very uncommon about it. It is never entered intentionally.

We can decide to clap our hands on the count of three, and do it every time. But if we decide to daydream on the count of three, what will happen? We can decide to daydream while letting that other part of our mind drive the car, but will it happen? *(I can sum-mon spirits from the vasty deep . . . But will they come?)*

The reason we have to acquire some kind of imagery induction, or self-hypnosis induction, is in order to put entering this semi–zone state under our voluntary control. At first, this may seem awkward and prolonged. At first, it is. One has only to think back to learning the golf swing to remember the same feeling. Whenever one acquires a skill that is not naturally easy to do there is an initial formality and awkwardness. It was true of the golf swing, and it is true of the zone-move, which frees us to make our range golf swing under pressure.

MAKING THE PRE-SHOT EFFECTIVE

This is the metaphor: You are outside a rented house in the cold. You want to get in. You carefully go through each of the keys on your ring to see if one of these strange things will open the door.

The motions of selecting and trying each key are the pre-shot routine. For an observer, such as the busybody neighbor across the street, the motions look the same whether the keys work or not. But if you do not have a key that works, you are still out in the cold. You have gone through the motions, yet you are still where you started. How often this happens on the golf course!

If you have a key that works, then you get into where you want to go. Self-hypnosis brushes the key and makes it work.

QUICK ZONE-MOVE TECHNIQUE:
RESET THE CHEMICALS

Sit comfortably in an easy chair or lie down on your own bed where you will not be disturbed.

Close your eyes and focus on your breathing. Sense the coolness of the air as it enters your mouth and lungs, and the warmth of the air as it leaves your body. (Entering, as it does, at room temperature and being exhaled at about 98 degrees—body temperature—it is, of course, warmer as it leaves.) Each time you exhale, silently say to yourself the word *relax*.

Now tense the muscles of the hands—make a fist and squeeze

tight to the count of three. Tight, tighter, relax. Let the hands go. Let the bed or chair support the hands.

Tense the muscles of the shoulders: tense, tenser, relax. Let the shoulders go.

Squeeze tight the muscles of the face. Hold this tightness to the count of three, then let the muscles of the face relax. Let the jaw drop down, mouth open, relaxed.

Squeeze tight the abdominals and the buttocks. Hold them tight to the count of three, then let them relax. Feel the chair or bed supporting the buttocks.

Tense the legs, tenser, as tense as you can, then relax.

While enjoying the feeling of relaxation, form your fingers in your customary grip on the golf club.

Think to yourself "When my fingers form this grip, my muscles will set themselves to this level of relaxation."

Then think to yourself "On the count of three, I will re-alert myself, feeling wide-awake, confident, and calm. Three, two, one, wide-awake."[2]

HOMEWORK Practice this technique for seven days, using an actual club for your grip prior to your pre-shot routine, and you will see tangible results. (Sorry, but there is nothing in golf that does not require practice.)

Relevance: If you have a repeating situation in which you release fight-or-flight chemicals, this is the exercise for you. If you get anxious on the first tee, or in the sand, or hitting over water, then this exercise will work wonders for your game.

Suppose that you habitually tighten up when you have to hit over water. What this means is that water has taken the place of the saber-toothed tiger in your mind. One million years ago you would wander out of the cave and when you encountered the saber-toothed

---

[2]If you experience any difficulty or problem whatsoever with your trial exercise, consult an appropriate professional.

tiger you would release fight-or-flight chemicals. Now you wander out of the clubhouse only to release fight-or-flight chemicals when you suddenly encounter water.

Clearly, water has become your traditional "enemy." The problem, of course, is that releasing these chemicals doesn't help you hit over water. You end up struggling to hit over water in spite of them. Indeed, perhaps because of them you will be unsuccessful from time to time in your effort to hit over water. But even occasional failure will be enough to ensure that you will produce these chemicals all the more in the future. The part of your mind that wants to protect you will be certain to produce these warning chemicals in the future.

This is easy enough to fix as long as you don't try to fix it in the intuitively obvious way. The intuitively obvious way is to tell yourself not to get anxious. That doesn't work. Nobody knows better that this doesn't work when hitting over water than those who tell themselves—as they are about to hit over water—not to get anxious.

It might be okay to tell yourself "don't get anxious" if that voice were in charge. But there is another boss in your head saying, "Watch out, there's water!"

The result is that now you have two bosses yelling at you, and, worse yet, they are yelling contradictory things. One is telling you that you are in serious danger, the other is telling you not to be anxious. You don't know what to do since you are supposed to obey your boss. The upshot is that you may get even more anxious! What's a golfer to do?

The answer is to bypass the bosses. Go to the back room where the chemicals are made.

This is one more time when it actually pays to have done your homework. Once you have done the *reset the chemicals* homework, you have the upper hand.

In the back room where the chemicals are made, you submit the order for the chemicals associated with the relaxation exercise. This acts not as a contradiction, but as a substitution.

You have effectively gone to the head of the line, and substituted a relaxation chemical order for what was to have been an anxiety chemical order. You have reset the mental computer to produce chemicals that correspond to the settings you have achieved in the relaxation exercise.

ADVANCED ZONE-MOVE TECHNIQUES

Imagery or self-hypnosis or zone-moves actually need have nothing to do with relaxation. The relaxation excercise is fine for establishing a relaxation setting, but it takes too long for golf purposes.

You are trying to be able to cue yourself to a specific mental state. But in certain situations, if your cueing is losing effect, you want to be able to recharge with a quick zone-move. The following forms the basis for an excellent approach.

USE ON THE COURSE

Obviously, on the course you do not want to be lying down or assuming odd positions. You don't need to.

You only need one or two seconds to reset the chemical dial in your favor. Pick your moment—and moments when no one is paying any attention to you are surprisingly common on the golf course. Our favorites are when someone else is preparing to tee off and when someone else is preparing to putt.

Both procedures take far more time than a resetting of the chemicals, and both procedures occupy the attention of everyone else.

Carry the appropriate club for the situation. If you are headed to the tee box, then of course you will be carrying your driver (or 3 wood). If you are approaching the green to putt, then you will be carrying your putter. As you walk let your right hand find the balance point near the head of the club, so that the weight of the club is almost evenly balanced on the fulcrum of your fingers, with your right hanging down naturally at your side.

Close your eyes and focus on the hanging weight of the club.

Wonder briefly if the club will stay perfectly balanced, but then feel the weight of the long handle slowly swing toward the ground. Sense that the handle going down opens a valve near your feet that allows tension and anxiety to flow down your body and out into the ground.

Focus on the tightness in your chest. Then sense that tightness and anxiety literally flowing down your body, through your legs and feet, and into the ground. Flowing like the old oil in your car when a mechanic opens the bolt that seals the crankcase. Just keep your eyelids shut until the tension and anxiety have flowed like a viscous liquid through your body into the ground.

If you like, you can visualize the needle on your internal tension meter sliding down in sync with your club handle to reach the settings you have practiced in your relaxation exercise. With practice, this zone-move takes several seconds, and is invisible to others.

This is a powerful secret weapon. Everyone else in your foursome has a backpack in which they are putting little stones of anxiety with every missed or disappointing shot. Most of the anxiety stones may be light enough. But the weight adds up. By the back nine they are carrying a heavy load of anxiety. Only you have a means of emptying the backpack, of getting rid of the anxiety.

If your range game is better than your course game, then this emptying of the anxiety backpack will make an enormous difference. It's hard to play your best when you are carrying all that weight. Look around. Most other people are carrying around a lot of weight, and are not playing their good range game. When you install a drain on the anxiety backpack, you go a long way toward separating yourself from the competition.

QUICK CURES

COMMON PUTTING PROBLEM

You can putt well enough. But sometimes, perhaps related to anxiety, you seem to lose your compass.

You are there on the green, bent over the ball, but you feel a little lost. You're not at all sure where to putt at. **Uncertainty** is the signal feeling in this situation. A number of directions and speeds all seem like they might be right.

You can spend eighteen (or more) holes in this woebegone state unless you do something about it. Or you can fix it in less than five seconds.

At the next convenient moment, close your eyes and go into your zone-state. Let the anxiety drain through your body into the ground. Then introduce the true statement "my hands know where to putt the ball."

Over the next ball, close your eyes for less than a second and repeat to yourself, "My hands know where to putt the ball." Then let your hands putt. Seeing is believing. You'll be pleased with the results.

COMMON DRIVING PROBLEM

Many players more or less (often less) approach the top, then suddenly feel an urge to hit the ball. *Rushed at the top* leads to many complications, and those lead to at least as many corrections or outright errors.

You may want to think of a comic strip we saw many years ago. In it there was a twenty-fifth hour on a special clock. We don't remember exactly how it worked, but basically those who got hold of the gizmo had access to this twenty-fifth hour in which all the rest of the world was stopped, and one could wander at will among these frozen statues, which would begin again when the twenty-fifth hour was up.

The plot of the comic had to do with the bad guys who wanted to loot and steal during the twenty-fifth hour, and the superhero who wanted to stop them.

You want to tell yourself that as your backswing approaches completion you enter the twenty-fifth hour. At the top you have all the time in the world. At the top time stands still.

This is one you can fix away from the golf course. Enter your zone-state in your spare time. Tell yourself that at the top of your backswing there is all the time in the world, at the top of your backswing Time Stands Still. Tell yourself that you will explore the twenty-fifth hour, and remain at the top for as long as you want.

And you will be telling yourself the truth. You will remain at the top of your backswing for as long as you want. Without that anxiety-induced rush at the top you will see your range swing emerge onto the course. And won't that be fun?

Custom Fitting

THERE ARE two parts to being a really good teacher. First, you have to know what parts of the student's swing you should leave alone. These are the elements that are highly functional—the parts that work—even if they are not aesthetically perfect.

Second, you have to know how to repair or eliminate those other elements that are hindering the swing.

Anyone with a good golf swing could simply tell the pupil to start over, and do everything in one particular way. Of course, this would be a long and frustrating process. It might not even be possible. More important, it would not be the way to get maximum improvement.

When Lee Trevino was a boy, some misguided pro could have taught him to swing like Sam Snead, or Ben Hogan, or Bobby Jones.

The end result might have been a gifted amateur with a pretty swing. But would we have ever heard of Lee Trevino? Probably not. Jim McLean makes a similar point in his excellent book, *Eight-Step Swing*, in which he introduces the valuable idea of a range of acceptable actions. There are, of course, a number of common elements in the swings of all great players—coupled with enough variation that every one of them can be recognized at a distance. Lee Trevino, Jim Furyk, Raymond Floyd, Arnold Palmer—these are clearly very distinctive. Nicklaus, Charles, Duval, Mickelson, Kite, Ballesteros, and anyone else you can think of has a swing as distinctive as a face or a fingerprint. It would be silly to say you have to learn to do exactly this or that in order to learn to swing. No two people have ever learned to do exactly this or exactly that in exactly the same way, which is why no two swings ever look exactly the same. (Although it is true that two swings made by the same pro player often look exactly the same; so if your own swings do not resemble each other closely, then you are not fulfilling that essential requirement identified by Ledbetter: the repeatable swing.)

Figuring out what can stay in the swing of the student is an art as well as a science, requiring a true understanding of golf swings. The sections on Driving, Sand, Chipping, and Putting include those elements that must remain in the swing. Of course, to remain they must have been there in the first place. Without these essential elements, it is meaningless to talk about psychological effects, because without them the swing will not be repeatable even in the total absence of anxiety or pressure. This book is about a swing that is repeatable on the range, about what happens to that swing when it is attacked by pressure, anxiety, fear, and anger on the course. And, of course, it is about how you can eliminate or reduce these psychological attacks (mental defenses), and how you can counter any attack that gets past your mental defense (physical defenses).

CUSTOM FITTING ISN'T ONLY FOUND IN GOLF

One should note that the idea that every great pro does many things differently from every other great pro is not peculiar to golf. John McEnroe's serve doesn't look like anything you would (or could) learn in a book, but it was dominant in his era. Sampras, Krajicek, and Martin are famous servers, but even a casual tennis fan would have no difficulty telling who was who with their backs to the camera. Again, there are subtle common elements that a good coach might work on, but there are large distinctive elements that a great coach would never change.

Ken Griffey, Jr., Mark McGwire, and Sammy Sosa are three great home-run hitters, but the point is the same: A great hitting instructor would rather eat the bat himself than ask one of these superstars to swing like another. Of course, that is obvious now because they are superstars, but a really great Little League instructor may have left the differences in place at that level, too.

Early on the great instructors distinguish between the idiosyncrasies that stand out to the naked eye but do not interfere with eventual success and those elements that must change before success can be achieved.

It may be as bad as to change something that is not interfering with performance as it is to ignore something that is actually causing a problem.

In fact, a rating system for professional instruction might theoretically be constructed in which all the necessary changes that are made successfully count for one point each, while all the arbitrary and unnecessary changes made count for minus one point. The great instructors, of course, are those with high positive scores.

Experts and accomplished students of the game know that what we have been saying about physical instruction is true. Some amateurs who have never taken a lesson, or have taken one or two before vowing "never again," may intuitively understand it also. There is little more frustrating than changing a few necessary and a few unnecessary things at the same time. A random dice-rolling element is introduced into the unfortunate player's game as, in the middle of an explosion on the course, he tinkers with sometimes relevant and sometimes irrelevant swing changes. The resulting inconsistency and sense of being out of control can frighten the student into abandoning instruction. The reliably frustrating is preferred over the surprise package, particularly when so many of the surprises are nasty ones.

PSYCHOLOGICAL DEFENSES NEED CUSTOM FITTING, TOO

As we have seen, great golf swings are different from each other (although with common elements). As we have also seen, great tennis serves and great home-run swings also are quite individualized. And this is true in every other sport as well. Joe Montana doesn't really look like John Elway when he throws the football. Scotty Pippen and Michael Jordan are both great basketball players, but from the back at fifty yards without numbers on their jerseys, you still know who is dribbling. Certainly coach Bill Parcells knows who is blocking in the game films without seeing the numbers on the Jets jerseys.

In one of the simplest of human physical endeavors (at least in the sense that everyone who tries to do it over time can do it adequately)— handwriting—every performance is distinct. Not only does no signature look like any other, but even a conscious and practiced attempt to imitate the physical performance of another (i.e., forgery) can be detected. Even in the simple sport of "handwriting," where there is some effort to teach everyone, at least in a given class or school system, to do it the same, they all look different. Yes, there are the necessary common elements—the Bs can't look like Ds, for instance—but any attempt to go beyond that would be both counterproductive and unsuccessful.

What very few people realize is that psychological defenses are individualized as well. Perhaps because we can't see them we are unable to appreciate how different one person's defenses are from another's.

As with physical instruction, it is as important to know what to leave in place as it is to know what to change.

There is no one exact way to defend against pressure and anxiety, just as there is no one exact way to hit the ball. If you could somehow sprinkle something in the air over every golfer's head that somehow made visible the "defenses" of great players who have done extraordinary things under pressure—let us imagine this magic powder made visible a colored aura around the heads of great golfers under pressure—then all of these colored auras would look different. That's right, no two would look alike! Just as the swings of great golfers look different from each other, so also would their defensive auras. And this is true for all the other sports as well: Just as the home-run swings of the great baseball players look different from each other, just as the serves of the great tennis players look different from each other, so also the defensive style of each of these players looks different from one another. They do have common structural elements, though, and they have a common and obvious bottom-line element as well.

The swings of great golfers, however different they look, all deliver a fast clubhead in a repeatable plane with a repeatable clubface angle (i.e., they all hit the ball well).

The defenses of great golfers, however different they would certainly look if made visible, nonetheless all eliminate fight-or-flight chemicals or reduce them to manageable levels repeatedly over time. Furthermore, all accommodate those chemicals that do slip by so that the shot is generally not ruined by the occasional stray burst of pressure chemistry.

For the psychological sports coach, also, it is as important to know what to leave in place as it is to know what to change. It is as counterproductive to change something that isn't interfering with good defenses as it is to leave in place something that is interfering with effective pressure reduction. Theoretically, sports psychologists could be graded with the same dual grading system we applied above to swing doctors. You get one point for every effective psychological defense you fix or add. You lose one point for every arbitrary or misguided psychological change you make to something that isn't interfering with the desired result.

In the physical realm, this is obvious. Sam Snead may have a "swing for the ages," but if a misguided Texas golf coach had long ago persuaded Lee Trevino to swing like him you would now be saying,

"Who's Lee Trevino?" General swing advice that does not take into account the particular swing of the particular player is doomed.

General psychological advice that does not take into account the particular psyche of the particular player is also doomed.

In the psychological realm, this is underappreciated, but one example makes it clear.

In the late seventies and early eighties, John McEnroe emerged as the best tennis player in the world. He was famous for his "tantrums," his acerbic dialogues with or at line judges or referees whom he felt (often correctly) had erred.

More than one commentator fell into the rather natural trap of opining that John was a good player, but that this kind of behavior could not help but interfere with his performance. "If he wants to be really successful, he's going to have to learn to take these things in stride" would be typical of comments he repeatedly elicited.

But nothing could be further from the truth!

He was wildly successful, in singles and in doubles. His "tantrums" didn't "get in his way." Far from it. He seemed to return to the game almost refreshed, focused and effective.

Would they work for you? Highly unlikely, just as Lee Trevino's swing would be unlikely to work for you. John McEnroe's defensive style has elements that are counterproductive for the overwhelming majority of people: They can't get back on track, as most people using Trevino's backswing can't get back on plane. But the fact remains that a sports psychologist who persuaded McEnroe to change his style at a young age would have done him, and tennis, a disservice.

Ironically, Bjorn Borg was just the opposite. On the court he was the ice man, showing no emotion. But Borg says that when he was young he had a terrible temper. After he had thrown his racket as a teenager, his parents didn't allow him to play for a period of time and told him that if he did that again there would be no more tennis at all. It seems intuitively obvious that for him this was the perfect intervention, as attested to by five Wimbledon titles and six French Open titles. It is fortunate that McEnroe and Borg weren't switched at birth.

Any psychology in which you must do exactly this or that can only succeed by chance. People are different and should feel free to employ a certain variety in their psychological game just as in their physical game. Just as many have been turned off golf instruction by an ineffective lesson, so have many others read or been told "you should always think of the color blue when you hit a good drive, then when you need a good drive think blue," or some such piece of advice. Many who try general advice get no benefit, and are turned off sports psychology altogether.

There are many ways to analyze the psychological game, just as there are many ways to approach the physical swing.

As with the physical swing, there are certain psychological fundamentals that should be observed. Beyond that there is a great deal of individual variation. The objective is to keep what does no harm, and to eliminate or fix whatever stands in the way of success.

There are many ways to talk about, to view, and to fix the swing (at the top, at impact, in terms of the arms, the legs, the pivot, the wrist-cock, timing, balance, swing plane—to name just a few). The student, by selecting that which is helpful, is somewhat intuitively keeping what works while discarding what doesn't work. With the help of a good instructor, he is able to do this sometimes more effectively and more efficiently.

There are likewise many approaches to psychological defenses. By presenting a variety of approaches and techniques, we enable the reader to intuitively select the effective while discarding the counterproductive. Of course, the help of a good sports psychologist or sports psychiatrist can sometimes accelerate this process, too.

But don't underestimate the enormous amount of good you can do yourself when you finally have a blueprint to psychological defense building. The "aura" of your psychological defenses is invisible, and so is air. At least in this case, the invisible exists, both for better and for worse. Both can do us great good and great harm. Air keeps us alive. It can keep us cool, but it can also blow our ball right into the hazard. Defenses are also invisible, but their effects are not. They can keep us cool under pressure, and we depend on them. Because without our defenses, as without air, we can choke.

25

What Is Your Mental Handicap?

THE WHOLE idea of handicap, of scoring average, of top-ten finishes is one of doing "more better, more often." We have known amateurs who were frustrated because they could (and had) parred each of the holes on an eighteen-hole course, so they were left wondering why they never shot 72, or anything even like 72. Similarly, a pro could birdie any particular hole on a course, but you don't see too many scores of 54 being posted.

The basic hope is that you will do better more often, not that you will do everything perfectly. This is equally true of the mental game. You cannot expect to be perfect mentally, to shoot a "mental 72" or a "mental 54." But you can improve your mental, as well as your physical, game over time, and play more better more often, with more enjoyment.

A useful concept is the **"mental par."** On any hole you can get a **"mental par,"** a **"mental birdie,"** or a **"mental bogey."** Obviously, if you throw your entire bag of clubs into the lake, you can get a "mental double bogey." If you hook it off the tee into the trees, but chip out and recover—focused and calm—you can score the "mental eagle."

Perhaps the greatest advantage of the **Mental Par** system is its implication. The implication is that if you mental bogey a hole, you can still mental birdie the following one. This is a supremely important concept.

People generally have the idea that you have mental game, or you don't. They know that physically you can play well on one hole and badly on the next. They know that the idea is to increase the number of holes on which you play well physically. They know this because physical play is visible.

But mental play is invisible and it is easy to subscribe to inaccurate ideas about it.

Mental play, like physical play, has its ups and downs. It is not true that people have it or they don't. As with physical play, some people are generally better (lower mental handicap) or worse (higher mental handicap). But as with physical play, on any particular hole the lower mental handicap player can do worse than the higher mental handicap player.

And your mental handicap, like your physical handicap, indicates how you do on average. Like your physical handicap, you can lower your mental handicap by doing better on average mentally on the golf course.

The ideal mental golfer brings his entire range game to the course. Even if his range game is the equivalent of a 21 handicap, if a 21 gets to the course then he is a scratch mental golfer. Conversely, if you hit like a 3 on the range, and play to an 8 on the course, then you are a 5 mental handicap. Your mental handicap is the number of strokes you have to add to your range game to accurately describe your course game.

Obviously, every stroke you take off of your mental handicap is also a stroke you take off of your physical handicap, since physical handicaps are calculated on the course. Equally obviously, your mental handicap is made up of how you do mentally over eighteen holes on multiple occasions. Players who let one bad mental hole fester into a series of bad mental holes will not have a low mental handicap.

They will not have a low physical handicap either.

26

Golf and Road Rage

YOU CAN hardly pick up the newspaper these days without reading about some new episode of what is called *road rage*. Legislatures are taking notice of this phenomenon. Police departments are establishing road rage hot lines and road rage task forces.

What is road rage? To understand the answer to that you have to be familiar with another modern word: *dis*. People with road rage are people who while driving a car feel they have been *dissed*. Someone cuts in front of them without leaving enough room. Or they are waiting in a turn-off lane and someone cruises down the other lane only to cut in front of them, rather than waiting their turn.

Then *kaboom*! These people blow their stack. They lose it. They go after the offender. They may follow the culprit honking the horn, or they may cut in front of the offender and then go deliberately slowly to punish the culprit. They may go ballistic and actually inflict damage for these transgressions with their car. They may ram the offender from the front, or the rear, or the side. They may even find a gun in their car and start shooting.

What's going on? And what does it have to do with golf?

Those are good questions, and this is the answer. But to understand the answer you have to get into the mind of the person with road rage:

I am driving down the highway. I have had a very hard day, but I am keeping it under wraps. I am following the speed limit because I am a good citizen (although I am in a big hurry to get home). I am waiting in the very long line to turn off onto my next highway, and I am perfectly aware that occasionally cars will cruise down the highway beyond the turn lane, then cut in. Though I want to get home, I would never do that because I know it isn't right. I always wait my turn.

Once I actually had a small accident while waiting to turn: I ran into the fender of the car in front of me, which was surprising. Surprising because I was only going three miles per hour.

Now, I am a good driver. I've never been in an accident, even while traveling at high speeds. How odd that I would have my only accident at three miles per hour!

Not so odd, just between you and me, because I was looking in the rearview mirror almost the whole time. And when I wasn't looking in the rearview mirror, I was looking in the side mirror.

Why was I looking behind me? Why wasn't I watching the road?

Well, that's a good question. I was looking for people who were going to cut in front of me. So that I could narrow up the space in front of me enough so that they wouldn't be able to cut in front of me.

And when they did, when something unfair happened to me— that's when I lost it.

Of course, the road rage people have nothing to do with us. Golfers aren't like them ... well, perhaps not entirely like them. But isn't there a little common ground?

Don't some golfers get upset when something "unfair" happens to them? In fact, some golfers are looking for "infractions." They come to the course searching for noise or movement during their swing, peering about for improperly raked traps or poorly manicured fringes. While no one likes to be taken advantage of, they have a particularly sharp eye out for balls rolled over and out-of-bounds lines not observed. A ball teed up in front of a marker, conferring little advantage, can make their day. The stronger the wish (which to the player's credit has been mastered) to gain an advantage, the greater the anger at others who have unfairly jumped ahead.

On a subtler level many more golfers are concerned about fairness from the elements, rather than from other players. They become upset when it "shouldn't" bounce back into the water, or lip out, or jump into the woods. In fact, doesn't almost everyone get upset when something unfair happens? Certainly, we all know people who are just waiting for something unfair to happen so they can complain, or lose it verbally, or bury a club.

There are early injustices that we carry with us. We are waiting for these injustices to occur again. If looking for what is unfair is the focus, then something will turn up. The bunker will not be raked, or will be short of sand. The ball will take an unlikely bounce into the water. The foursome on the next green will shout in your backswing. We saw in a previous chapter the many ways we try to exorcize an old sense of unfairness by pointing the finger at a culprit in the present.

This borders on another way golf is like life. People want to have their cake and eat it, too. People want the course to be exciting and challenging, but they want it to be perfectly fair. The two don't go together. A perfectly flat sod farm might have no unfair bounces, but who would want to play it? Meanwhile, every day on every golf course in the world some ball is taking an unexpected bounce into a trap or water, and some player is complaining that it is "unfair." There is a clear corollary in life.

In life, men and women will tell you they want to go out with someone "exciting," then they will sometimes complain that the exciting person turned out to be unreliable or untrustworthy. And when they're introduced to someone trustworthy and reliable, they will complain that he or she is "boring," or, in modern parlance, that there is "no chemistry."

In life, a hotel room might be expensive or economical; the expensive hotel room might be on the beach with an ocean view while the smaller but more economical room overlooks the Interstate. Well, that makes sense. One way you get more of one thing (savings), the other way you get more of the other (luxury).

What doesn't make sense is to insist on saving money and then complain bitterly about the view. That makes no more sense than to insist on the ocean suite and sulk about the price.

The top-of-the-line SUV costs more than the sedan. We don't buy the Navigator and then go home in sticker shock, because we know that the two—size and price—are part of a package, just as we don't buy the subcompact, then complain that we can't tow a trailer offroad in the Rockies.

These examples are obvious, though even they can create some conflict in all of us. But the further we move from concrete examples where "what you get" and "what it costs" are clearly spelled out, the more conflict and anxiety and error are created by this type of choice.

This is unfortunate because in life (and in golf) choices of this type are everywhere. An employment opportunity with more upside may offer less security. The Internet stock could really take off; whereas, while you are not going to get rich quick off the Treasury bill, you also aren't going to lose your money. If you open your own business the sky is the limit, but if you work for the government or a large corporation you are more likely to collect a paycheck every week.

In a sense, the conflict is between hope and fear. We hope for something (big returns, great success, wild happiness) while at the same time we fear something else (going bust, total failure, loneliness and loss). And as we have seen, the more we go for the big return, the more we risk the big failure. While the safer we play it—the more we minimize our chances for loss—the less chance we have of scoring big. Sound familiar?

Of course it does. It sounds like golf. The more we go over the trap right at the pin, the better our chance for the bird. But the safer we play it—going for the center of the green and taking the trap out of play—the more we avoid the risk of bogey. Really whacking it off the tee has enormous upside, putting us in scoring position. Playing safe off the tee avoids tremendous downside: sand, water, rough, trees, or out-of-bounds. If you really go for that snaky downhill eight-footer you have a chance of making it *and* a chance of 3-putting.

Jill has been going out with Bob for over a year. Secretly, she had always thought she would marry someone more dynamic, better looking, and more successful. But they get along well, or at least they get along well enough that she doesn't know what to do. She hates to admit it but she would like more; yet she doesn't want to break up with Bob and lose what she has.

Jim finds Kate unbelievably attractive, but they argue a lot. She is critical of the long hours he works, and not all that happy about the amount of time he spends on the weekends playing golf. But she comes from a good family, and when things are good they are great. He would like something more (someone who looked just like her but who adored him the way he is). However, experience has led him to believe that if he breaks up with her, he may not only deeply regret it, he may also end up with someone rather measurably worse.

Jim and Jill both want to go for it, but they don't want to make a mistake. The "perfect" mate would constitute a birdie, but going for it would entail the bogey risk of bad outcome (loneliness, worse mate).

Married couples who contemplate separation or divorce often face the same fundamental, difficult calculation: "I would like to end up better off than I am, but I would hate to end up worse off than I am now." Since 50 percent of marriages end in divorce, it is fairly certain that on any given day there are a lot of people agonizing over the hope of getting a better outcome in life (mate who loves/under-stands/cares) while grappling with the fear of a worse outcome (lone-liness, separation from children, worse mate).

And at any given moment during daylight hours there are count-less golfers on the tee, near the trap, beside the water, or on the green, all over the courses of every country in the world who are struggling with the forces of the Basement saying, "Go for it," while the Up-stairs is warning, "Don't make a mistake."

We are not attempting to trivialize the many difficult life deci-sions that parallel the perennial golfer's struggle between hope and fear. Rather, the opposite is true.

To the extent that we can trivialize the golfer's dilemma, or at least reduce the flow and effect of anxiety chemicals engendered by that dilemma, then we improve the golfer's game (shrink his handi-cap) and at the same time enlarge his enjoyment.

It is true that when we feel a conflict between hope and fear, we produce anxiety chemicals, both in life and on the golf course.

Anxiety is not helpful in resolving our dilemmas. In many ways, this maladaptive defense mechanism of unwonted anxiety is better repaired on the golf course: while the same chemicals are engendered as in dangerous situations, there is in reality no danger. We cannot end up dead, broke, or alone on the golf course. We react as if saber-toothed tigers were alive on the course because we bring our reac-tions from the rest of life and superimpose them on golf. Our anxieties and fears from the past and the present pervade and poison our game. The good news in the next section is that not only can we rescue our golf game, at the same time we can improve the quality of the rest of our life.

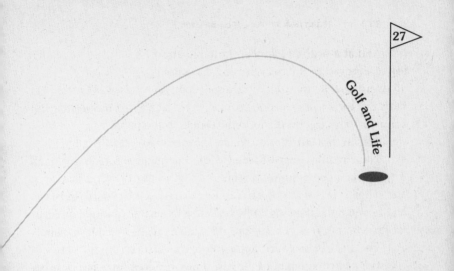

A LOT of basketball players who can make a particular shot in practice have trouble in a game. And on a more elite level, players who can make the shot in the first period have trouble with the game on the line, two seconds on the clock. Why is that?

In practice we have our range game, dominated by hope and enthusiasm from the caveman in the Basement. We know what we want, and we go directly about getting it.

With the game on the line, we also have fear. We have the directives from the Upstairs not to make a mistake, not to mess up. These are not helpful thoughts. As we have seen, when the Basement wants us to go for it, and the Upstairs doesn't want us to make a mistake, then the Ground Floor doesn't know what commands to send, and anxiety chemicals are produced.

"Don't give them anything to hit but don't walk anybody" is an old baseball joke. It typifies the bind of the player who must do well but who must not make a mistake.

In tennis you want a winner, but you don't want an unforced

error. Similar to the basketball example above, it will be a lot easier to hit winners in practice than at match point.

And in golf you want a great shot, but you don't want a mistake. On the range, where you don't care all that much about mistakes, it will be easier to hit a good shot. On the course, and especially in a pressure situation on the course, there will be directives from the Upstairs.

The caveman in the Basement of your mind wants to go for it. The Upstairs containing the combined teachings of parents, teachers, and religion tells us to be careful not to make a mistake. Enthusiasm and hope and aggression come from the Basement. Caution and fear of making mistakes come from the Upstairs.

The struggle between hope and fear is essential to all sports. It is also a key component of the rest of life. And any struggle between hope and fear produces anxiety.

Many people perform less well than they could ideally in any situation in which they feel any level of anxiety. The caveman chemicals, as we have seen, don't help on the golf course, and they don't help in the rest of life either.

Public speaking, auditions, job interviews, dating, sex, and many other activities provide an opportunity for fight-or-flight chemicals to interfere with our ability to perform. Every day we see saber-toothed tigers where they are not, and the chemicals flowing through our bodies from this false sighting cause us to tighten up. The more we hope to do well while at the same time fearing to do badly, the more anxiety chemicals we will have.

Our "range game" is a concept not limited to the game of golf. In life, too, there is a certain level of ability that we are able to show when we are not threatened.

If we can speak clearly and convincingly to one or two people but struggle more in front of a large audience, then we are having a problem bringing our public speaking "range game" to the course.

If we are natural with our friends but artificial on a first date, then the same thing is true. If this only happens when we care about the man or the woman, then we are seeing a saber-toothed tiger only in the situation in which we are afraid of losing.

The mental handicap is an extremely useful concept in life as well as in golf. You will recall that this is the difference between the score you would get on the course if you were playing your "range game" and the score you actually get. Mental handicap is the measure of the extent to which anxiety chemicals bring down your game.

In life events we have a predictable extent to which anxiety chemicals will affect our performance. The difference between how well you speak to one or two people and the way in which you give the speech to a large audience is, in the "sport" of public speaking, your mental handicap. Decreasing your mental handicap allows you to come closer to performing at your maximum level, in public speaking or any other human endeavor.

The hazards on the golf course act on us like the hazards in life. The man who cannot be as natural and likeable on a first date with a woman he wants to impress can have the same fears of not doing well in his golf life when confronted by sand and water. The woman who is afraid to stand up and speak in front of others may also have concerns about teeing off in public. If you have trouble closing a deal, you may also have trouble closing out a hole with a short putt.

There are numerous symbolic obstacles on a golf course; they symbolize the obstacles we encounter in life. As in life, they are often in the short run unfair, and we can focus on that unfairness. Our inability to deal with obstacles gracefully on the golf course can lead to avoiding playing with strangers or in public, avoiding competition, or avoiding the game altogether.

We can similarly contrive to speak to small groups we know; we can date only "sure things." Or we can avoid public speaking altogether, or complain about the unfairness of dating.

Or we can focus on overcoming the obstacles to achieve what we want. In life as in golf, instead of running away from situations that cause anxiety chemicals, we can work to diminish the production and effect of these anxiety chemicals: We can lower our mental handicaps.

One of the great lessons of behavior therapy is that when we lower the flow of anxiety chemicals in one situation, then the flow from other "saber-toothed tigers" is likewise diminished. This is great news! We have previously seen that resolving certain conflicts in life or correcting certain ways of thinking will reduce misplaced production of anxiety chemicals on the golf course.

The opposite is true as well. Reducing the flow of anxiety chemicals on the golf course will carry over into life. The flow of unnecessary anxiety chemicals in various situations in life will be decreased by tightening the anxiety faucet on the golf course!

When we lower our mental handicap on the golf course, we lower it in the rest of our life as well. The boardroom, the bedroom, the backgammon table, and the back nine have this in common. Lower your mental handicap and you will have the pleasure of being able to say, "Hello, Range Game."

People will say to you "Do your best," but that is hapless and ineffective advice. On the other hand, when you lower your mental handicap, when you decrease the flow of anxiety chemicals, then you approach actually doing your best. Having the best that you can do appear upon your command—well, what more can you ask for?